Belfast: City of Light

Looking and Listening to Belfast, Come with Me

Belfast: City of Light

Looking and Listening to Belfast, Come with Me

Bronagh Lawson

Published by Inner Stream Ltd
2019

Inner Stream Ltd
City East Business Centre
69-72 Newtownards Road
Belfast
BT4 1GW
Northern Ireland
Email: innerstreamltd@gmail.com

First Published 2019

Paperback ISBN: 978-1-9163089-0-9

eBook ISBN: 978-1-9163089-1-6

To Norbert and Leo

Contents

Acknowledgements

I would like to thank my husband Norbert for his support and outsider view point which has always been crucial to me. My ancestors for ensuring that I was born into the right time in the right place. To Ganger who taught me to appreciate the unseen world. My mother Frances who supported me and all my sisters to try and reach our potential. My father Paddy who never accepted the status quo. The people of Portaferry and Strangford who taught me what community is all about, and the people of Belfast I came across in my development work, who shared their struggles while simply trying to improve their lot. To Seedbed Belfast that understood that it's individuals that can really change things.

To Dr Grace Clunie and Rev Johnston McMaster who were the first people to view my initial book drafts. Fidelma Carolan, Joanne Bunting MLA, Rev Ruth Patterson, Rev Harold Good, Martin Donnelly, Brian Irvine, Alistair MacLennan, Father Martin Magill, all gave me interesting vital perspectives in the final two years of development, and Emeritus Professor Pauline Murphy who encouraged me to simply finish the book. To the artists of Belfast who dream of other worlds and lastly to my sister in subversion Adjunct Professor Suellen Semekoski at the School of Art Institute Chicago, without whose lifetime's experience and dedication to the world of art and spirit none of this would have made sense.

Preface

I did not set out to go on this journey or write this book but simply started to follow an artistic thread like many artists over the centuries before me. The thread became so compelling and extraordinary that I eventually felt destined to write it down.

What if instead of listening to the continuous repeated stories of Protestant vs Catholic in Belfast, an individual had first-hand experience of visiting every church in the city for a service, simply looking and listening when going to each one?

What would they see and hear? As a non-churchgoer starting out on this journey, how would you feel ten years later? What is going on in Churches in contemporary Belfast?

How might this open-minded curiosity inform the continuous shifting conversation about the city that I call home?

Introduction

It seems that if you take any snapshot of time in Ireland's, Northern Ireland's and the United Kingdom's history it acts as a continually unfolding narrative of complexity. For hundreds of years the geopolitics of the islands has troubled many and incited violence in others; the fight or flight mechanisms have been bred into us natives because of real first-hand experience of violence or the threat of it. It can take time to switch off from those violent impulses.

In the 60's the Troubles, traditionally reported as a conflict between Protestants and Catholics in which over 3,600 people died, broke out in Northern Ireland and for thirty years bombs and bullets were an everyday occurrence in the streets of Belfast and beyond. The peace process since has been an elaborate dance of two steps forward and one step back with innumerable complicated accounts evolving all the time with the Good Friday Agreement at the core.

We're only a little region of the world measuring just under fourteen thousand square kilometres with a population of around 1.8 million that is still learning to govern itself with much distrust and not much leeway. Yet somehow relative peace has come to our shores and we would like to keep it that way. The chronic nature of violence in the past and the close proximity of victims and perpetrators has meant that peace has been difficult to keep on track but still many try. While others try to flip it back into violence. To me, however, there is always a feeling that we must try harder to move towards true peace.

I am heartened that the European visitors staying with me for a short while in Belfast have never heard of the IRA (Irish Republican Army) or the UVF (Ulster Volunteer Force) or any of the breakaway groups, and that the daily happenings of violence have mostly become a bad memory that are for some more vivid than others.

We are left with Belfast, the capital of Northern Ireland or the north of Ireland, being known as the trauma capital of the world, so where do we go from here, and is there something we have missed?

Chapter 1: In the Beginning

"Would anyone like to go to church?" asked my friend Martha.

We were in Dublin and had just woken up after a fancy-dress party for a friend's fortieth. Many of the revellers staying overnight had surfaced for breakfast and were nursing hangovers.

"Yes, I'll go," was my response. I thought the walk would do me good before driving back to Belfast.

It was a Catholic church – quick service, rhythmic mumbling prayers and automatic responses. The congregation knew the drill and enjoyed the haste. The surprise for me was a feeling that I'd had previously being amplified a hundredfold within this church, during the service. Great flows of something – energy maybe would be the best way to describe it, trickled down my head. On exiting the church, I turned to Martha and told her what had happened.

She said, "Maybe we're converting you?"

"No, I don't think so, but something's up," I replied.

Religion and I didn't really get on. In my first year at grammar school my school report showed my religion mark to be nineteen per cent and my class position to be eighty-eight out of ninety. The teacher's comment was "Uninterested", and quite honestly that is how I stayed for the next thirty-five years.

Before undertaking this journey, I would have described myself as spiritual but removed, by choice, from the mainstream religions in Northern Ireland. In my teenage years I built up a barrier between myself and religion; a result of what I saw on a daily basis during the Troubles – people being blown up, murdered and all nature of horrific incidents – something to do with God apparently. If it hadn't been for my paternal grandmother, "Ganger" or Anna Lawson, who had a very strong faith, I don't think I'd even have been christened or confirmed.

Having been born in the sixties and brought up in rural Northern Ireland, the Troubles and endless Protestant versus Catholic violence and rivalry just switched me off to a true connection to any church. I blocked out what was going on to survive, tried to be a normal teenager and planned my escape to England and art college. In later years I was disgusted by what had happened in Northern Ireland in the name of religion, and as every church scandal broke out in the media I revelled in its reporting because it seemed to confirm my, and no doubt others, thoughts that organised religion was best avoided; that it was more about abuse and subjugation than love. The height of my church attendance was carol services, weddings, christenings, funerals or European Heritage Open Days, where I would simply enjoy the quietness of the space. Nothing, I thought, would get me to engage any differently.

Put off by my early experiences of religion and not being one for scripture union where they all seemed a little smug and suspiciously happy, I grew up with the constant reminder of the connection between religion and violence and hid in the art room at any opportunity, dreaming of another life. Living in the country it felt as if the action was happening down the road, over the next hill, far enough away, and many people just tried to get on with their lives as best they could. I attended a school with ninety-eight per cent of pupils from one religion but had a wide selection of village friends from the "other side". Always mixing, I was never one of those Northern Irish people who didn't know someone from another religion until they went to third-level education, if they were lucky enough to get there.

I escaped to art college in England in the eighties and thought I'd never again live in Northern Ireland full-time, but after years in Bristol, Winchester, London and then New York on a Fulbright Scholarship I found myself back in Northern Ireland pre-ceasefire. Someone recently asked me why I came back – after all it was still pretty dangerous, but it's hard to describe just how normal it was to exist with some level of violence. It was the elephant in the room, a constant presence and topic of conversation that many people were expert in living around.

The ceasefire happened while I and twenty-five other Northern Irish twenty-eight-year olds were on a Wider Horizons programme, funded by the International Fund for Ireland, in Thunder Bay, Canada. The initiative was through Townsend Enterprise Park in Belfast and Dundalk Unemployment Resource Centre, over the border, and it was aimed at young people who were looking to set up their own business.

We couldn't quite believe the news, but felt optimistic and energised about the future on our return, which all the northern participants decided to do – make a go of it at home. This wasn't easy. Many people told me just to leave, but although I knew people lived differently elsewhere, as I'd experienced it myself, I really wanted to be back in Northern Ireland; it was home after all. Many of the group met on a Friday to give each other peer support and encouragement. We called it "That was the week that was …" and would share the highs and lows of the previous five days; vital sustenance at a difficult time.

I remember saying to George Briggs, one of the mentors on the programme, that I would like his job. Taking me seriously he took me under his wing when we returned from Canada and I set about becoming a trainer-cum- mentor-cum-business advisor. In the following thirteen years I spent my time designing and running cross-border cross-community development programmes, mostly within the Enterprise Park network; moving people into voluntary, full- or part-time work, education or self-employment. I wanted to contribute to the much-needed mental shift and peace-building work happening and found I had a knack for it. People would say to me, "Oh, you're not making anything creative anymore," and I'd reply, "Do you know how creative you have to be, standing in a training room on a peace line trying to get people to focus on their cashflows while there's a paramilitary funeral going on outside?" I loved the people but found great difficulty with the systems of "support", not understanding at the time that they were traumatized.

The end of my work in north Belfast – which at the time had the five most-deprived wards in Europe, came when I walked into work one day and collapsed, no more able to process what I later understood to be the trauma of the people I was dealing with on a daily basis and the aggressive, violent spirit of the place. After some time off I returned to work and handed in my notice, unwilling to put my body through the continuous stress of working in such an environment. My boss, Michael McCorry, died of lung cancer a year later, brought on no doubt by the stress of developing a business centre from the ground up in a contentious interface area. Some everyday questions he had to answer were, "Can we build a twelfth of July bonfire in your car park?", "What shall we do with the pipe bomb I found in the shrubbery?" and the classic, "How are we going to get the tiles back on the roof – the ones we saw on the news being pulled off and thrown in the road during rioting?"

In north Belfast I marvelled at what was happening there in order to try and keep it safe; while at the same time I noticed how disconnected Belfast was – with people living in those "safe" areas seemingly wanting to hold onto their positions of privilege and look down their noses at the parts of Belfast that had been deeply immersed in conflict. In the past, granted, this was for safety reasons, but was that still relevant? Some people would ask me why I would take on such roles? But somebody had to.

Three years after leaving North City Business Centre I started to feel like I was getting back to my old self. I worked freelance training and mentoring but found the pull towards spending time connecting with the creator and maker in me overwhelming. The essential nature of me – what I had pursued as a girl, like other artists before me, obsessed for hours over the deep meditative nature of the creative process, but my connection had been clogged by vicarious trauma. A Wikipedia definition of which is:

> "A transformation in the self of a trauma worker or helper that results from empathic engagement with traumatised clients and their reports of traumatic experiences. It is a special form of counter transference stimulated by exposure to the client's traumatic material. Its hallmark is disrupted spirituality, or a disruption in the trauma workers' perceived meaning and hope. The term was coined specifically with reference to the experience of psychotherapists working with trauma survivor clients."

It gives you an idea of what I and others were dealing with on a day-to-day basis and aids understanding in what happened to me.

My creativity was belittled by a society desperately trying to be post-conflict, but getting back to creating my own artwork intensively after using my creativity for other things is a sublime experience. I was being called to stop what I was doing and make some space for making and creating again, and once I started, I couldn't stop. "Stop" and "create" are two of the most powerful words I know.

4

History is littered with artistic souls who have pursued the goal of creative expression, ignoring advice and family pressures to follow the creative muse wherever it drags itself. It's an obsession like no other that keeps the artist awake at night dissatisfied with mere reality. For who decides what reality is? Wherever creativity demands to be taken, the frustration and joy that can be found in creative expression equals nothing else I've ever come across. For those who know, the experience of creating something from nothing takes great courage – often it's not compatible with family life, and a complete disaster for the finances, yet still create an artist must. Without it they are doomed to simply repeat what has gone before. The artist has a unique role to disrupt thinking and space for something other. Perhaps that's why we are often pushed to the edges – we're seeking new shores.

Learning printmaking became an obsession and the world of cash flows and contracts retreated to a distant memory as I disappeared into my own artwork. Still working part-time as a business advisor, it became more and more difficult to switch out of creative mode. From time to time I got a feeling of quietness and calm, like all the world becoming silent, and an energetic trickling flowed down my head, similar to the feeling I got in that Dublin church. There was no logic to it – it would happen randomly while printmaking, driving or walking across fields. It was happening enough to mention to my husband who replied with, "Do you think you need your head examined?" The energy seemed friendly and good but what exactly was it?

It's worth noting that I wasn't the best person to be around at this time. I had financial pressures and a need to work for financial reward, yet my inner essence was demanding to create for its own sense. I couldn't articulate it then but I see it now in my artwork completed around that time. Nothing was standing in my way of a return to myself; no expectations, no other demands were more important. It was great to connect with the artistic community of Belfast, and to realise that there was an underground of artistic activity pulsating through the city – alive if not totally well. I admired their tenacity, their demand to create whatever the difficult circumstances and the lack of opportunity for their output.

Does inner essence need explaining? Do you have an inner life? Have you ever been quiet enough to consider if you have an inner world? My inner world of imagination was developed from an early age. Along with my three sisters I created drawings, paintings, plays, games, other worlds. It continued at school and into art college and beyond. For me, when I was working in North City Business Centre every half hour was regulated, every client I met was another demand on my knowledge base – statistics, databases to keep up to date. In stolen moments I drew in diagram form how I saw the policies of the interface and whether they were working or not. Clients' issues whirled around my head days after seeing them – even on holiday it took four days to unravel my mind from work issues. When I finally returned to myself and allowed some quiet time, I was too tired to create. Sometimes I sketched something but the output was more insipid than what was in my mind. I was caught up in life.

At the core of the main spiritual traditions is the practice of sitting still to allow the mind to settle and deal with what's arising. It's a simple exercise that can be undertaken in the physical body anywhere. Sublime. Artists and monks are two of the few groups of humanity who still hold this premise at their heart. This is where I was at on attending the service in Dublin. Suddenly there was a very specific amplification of the experience in a church – but what was it and what did it mean? The experience unsettled me and stayed in my mind.

I started to look at how many churches there were around where I lived in east Belfast, a majority Protestant area; ones I had driven or walked past on many occasions. Was it just that church in Dublin or was it every church that would give me the same experience? If so, how could it be explained? What exactly had I stumbled upon?

A couple of weeks later I found myself getting up on a Sunday morning and going to the closest church to my house. There are quite a few to choose from – six within a fifteen-minute walk and another twenty within a fifteen-minute drive. I was genuinely surprised at how many people were in attendance – in my secular world I thought no one really went to church any more.

For a couple of months, I continued to explore the churches around me, not every week but enough to worry my husband, a non-

6

churchgoer. I kept thinking, I'm not really going to church, am I? I became fascinated by what people were doing: do I sing? Sit or kneel, do either? Do people talk to me? What are people wearing? How many collections are there? Am I invited to have coffee afterwards? Who else is there? What are they saying? Do you need to wear a hat? I started to jot down my findings in a notebook combining them with anything I was handed – newsletters, hymns sheets, barbecue invites, calendars.

I must make it clear that if you had ever told me I'd be doing this in my forties, I would have fervently denied it, pleaded insanity and ran for the hills. Churches annoyed me, I had no intention of exploring it further and would roll my eyes and swear loudly at the suggestion. Even the word "God" annoyed me. Why? Because of how I had heard it being used previously – for wars, land grabs, murder, subjugation of women, the list goes on and on. When admitting to myself I was going to pursue my interest further, I had no plan, didn't feel compelled to go at a certain time every Sunday, got up when I felt like it and went to whatever church was starting around that time, but I did develop a loose formula that has been suggested to be a 'spirit-led' approach to my investigation:

- If anyone talked to me, I told them the truth about what I was doing;
- If possible, I didn't look at the denomination before entering and tried to guess once I was inside;
- If I took photographs, I asked someone in the church first and always took them after a service;
- When there was something going on politically in an area, I tried to visit a church there that week;
- I always had a hat handy (I later ditched this rule);
- I entered into the spirit of the worship;
- I noted down my observations as soon as possible afterwards;
- If anyone told me about a particular church, I tried to go there soon after;
- I made up my own boundary around Belfast;
- I could stop any time I got bored.

It's worth noting that during this time I had an artist studio in City East, a building at the bottom of the traditionally loyalist Newtownards Road across the road from the republican Short Strand area of east Belfast. The building itself had taken over ten years to negotiate before building started because of the fractious and contentious nature of the area. I was given space in return for some artwork and running an exhibition in the building. I needed the time and space to see what arose, and it's where I completed a body of work called *The Ebb and Flow of East Belfast*, a series of over a hundred etchings based on the area. It was an important step in my journey.

As a development worker in north Belfast I had often sat in my office thinking about everything that was going on around me, and the way the powers that be were trying to develop the area – perhaps with a riot starting outside – wondering what exactly was going on and how it was ever going to be resolved. During that period there were endless demands on my time and a constant flow of people requiring help and further direction, mostly with dark clouds hanging over them. I often got the feeling I was the first positive, hopeful person they had come across, and I was always surprised by the positive results I got with people simply by being logical and supportive.

This time it was different. I had a studio and no one was knocking at my door for anything. The time was all mine and I intended to use it to figure something out – what, I'm not entirely sure – a fresh way of depicting the peculiarity that is Northern Ireland eventually became the answer.

When out and about on a Sunday in Belfast, I often dropped into the studio to write up that morning's findings and enjoy the peaceful nature of the bottom of the Newtownards Road on a commuter car-free day.

I didn't set out to do anything other than see if I could find out more about this trickling feeling, and saw it merely as an artistic investigation that I could stop at any time, but my previous experience of cross-community work made me realise there was much more to it. The statement of Protestants vs Catholics or vice versa was so often heard and unchallenged as an opening communication for many a conversation or declaration. But what if there was a first-hand

8

experience of what this meant in a contemporary environment? Would it be knowledge that could inform a different kind of dialogue? And if so, what would that knowledge be?

Chapter 2: Early On in the Investigation

Who do churchgoers vote for? And why on earth do they still attend church? I was part of the secular liberal artistic community, which of course was the way forward, so I couldn't understand how people could still be going to church after all the suffering it caused.

It was a frosty morning but I thought I might just walk out of the house, turn right and see which church I came across first that was open. In I went. The congregation was a small but devoted group of around fifteen people. As soon as I entered the main room I had the feeling of being plugged into something from the middle of my head, and all the other people in the room being plugged in as well. Oh, dear, what was happening? I looked around at everyone, the people were not a group I had ever come across in other spheres of my life. It was really cold – is that why the women still had their hats on and people were sat around the radiators at the edges? Realising a hat was the dress code, I slipped on my woolly hat and the service started. Welcomed as a stranger, I was directed from the pulpit.

It was the first church service I'd ever been at where a collection wasn't taken. On investigating this afterwards, I found that if a collection isn't taken at a church service there's usually an offering box somewhere for people to leave their contribution. At one service, however, I was told I couldn't make an offering as it was considered a privilege and only available to full members of the church. I found two churches that have two collections one in Ballymurphy and one on the Newtownards Road where people go up in front of the congregation and give in front of everyone.

Each time I stepped over a church threshold into a service I was unaware of what I might find and sometimes it made me even more confused. For a start, were they all actually talking about the same thing? When should I sit or stand? Did I feel out of place? Was it obvious I wasn't one of the congregation – a sinner and heathen interloper? I began taking seats towards the back because at least I could see the people in front of me and follow their lead. Which prayers are where? Do you get a book? What page is this on? Where's the order of service? Do I sing now? Is that the right hymn – the right verse – on the overhead projector or is the projectionist asleep? What do you mean you only sing every other verse! What about Psalms – sing or read? All or every other verse? Do people know this is not the faith I was brought up in? What are all these Creeds?

The rituals and liturgy of each church had a unique slant, their own way of doing things, of interpreting the world of the spirit differently. All this against a backdrop of secular consumerism and the historical burden of religion in Northern Ireland, which sometimes seemed at odds with basic teachings. This, as well as my own spiritual imprint, stamped upon me with all the intergenerational baggage that goes along with it and being brought up in a time of conflict, even if I was very much on the margins; these were some of the thoughts whirling through my head for the first couple of years.

What about inside the church – was it wallpapered or decorated? Plain? Was there any stained glass? Did it have seats, pews or benches – standing room only? Whatever was going with each physical church and service, it was clear it was having some sort of bodily effect on me. Sometimes I could feel a dragging from my insides like something was pulling or unravelling against my will. I felt compelled to draw images over and over of how this felt to try and make some sort of sense out of it. I removed myself from much of mainstream life; with no TV for fifteen years I took to real life, church, studio, art exhibitions. I even stopped having a mirror in the bathroom after it was refurbished and enjoyed the lack of self-criticism this resulted in. Belfast was shifting and so was I.

One day the quiet inside my being felt so sublime and the radio in the car so noisy with static that when I switched it off, I felt as if I had slipped into a parallel universe. Instead of avoiding people giving away tracts or religious literature on the streets I stopped and chatted with them, looking at the different ways people try to share a religious tradition – or was it brainwashing? As the scales fell from my eyes, I could see an invitation to connect everywhere.

A knock at my door was the Latter-day Saints, two young men sharing the Word. I told them what I was doing and they explained which church they were connected to. I promised to visit in the coming weeks. They recognised me when I entered their temple and after the service came for a chat. During the service itself, I found it interesting that two members of the church researched different passages of the Book of Mormon and talked about them in relation to their own lives. The congregation called each other sister and brother. In our chat afterwards I was introduced to some congregants. The two young men told me I was the only one who smiled at them and didn't close the door in their faces the day they knocked. For the amount of rejection they received, they seemed to have amazing resilience. At another Latter-day Saints church in another part of the city I asked how they decided which doors to knock on. They had the whole city mapped out and did it bit by bit, but they wouldn't knock on the doors in west Belfast. When I asked why they just shook their heads.

It happened again: walking into the church I was welcomed by a number of people at the doorway who smiled and shook hands with me. I took the Bible and hymn book and found a seat. The decor was a mixture of old and new, with artefacts dotted around the room, obviously from another era. "Hello, I'm Pat, can I sit here?" asked the smiling lady beside me. We got chatting. Pat had attended the church for over twenty years, and though living away from the estate she still liked to come back to it. Now, however, she was moving to Bangor and so would shift churches as well. Her husband was ill, she said, and she had more family down in Bangor. This conversation is not remarkable in itself – just one human connecting with another, telling of personal issues, sharing with a stranger.

After this particular service Pat told me that the church was once blown up in the 1990s. A large bomb nearby had damaged all three churches in the area, as well as a thousand homes. She let out a nervous laugh as she talked about it, still fresh in her head. Strangely, the large lit-up cross on the side of the church stayed illuminated after the bomb exploded and a photo still hangs in the church to remind the congregation of this.

I was invited to stay behind for tea and seven people came to speak to me. Declining the tea, I thought again how nice it was for the church to offer the fellowship of hospitality after the service. As the congregation lingered, I looked deep into the eyes of these faithful followers and could see the difference that the church made in their daily lives: their eyes glowed and their presence vibrated. What on earth was it?

As I drove off, again I marvelled at the fact that there were three different denominations of churches on one housing estate, all within a short walking distance of each other. Some online research showed that the bomb was in 1992 with first reports of seven hundred homes damaged. Exaggeration developing over time, I thought, until I came across other reports stating that over a thousand homes were damaged in the estate (don't be so quick to judge, Bronagh!).

I lived in Northern Ireland at the time yet have no recollection of it – blanked out and filed with the other atrocities our city has witnessed. Twenty-seven years have passed, yet the memory is still clear in this congregation's mind. When will the memories end or be transformed? Should they be? I'm struck by how much in common churchgoers of any denomination have over the secular world outside. That whether they speak to me or not, all these congregations around the city are fighting off a secular malaise that's happening on the outside. It's maybe not as strong in Northern Ireland as it is in other parts of the UK and Ireland, but relevant all the same and pulsing through our daily media output around and about us. How can people be encouraged to see what I've seen and experienced – an alternative view of the spiritual life of the city?

After a service in Saint George's Anglican Church one day, I asked someone what the streams of light were called in the mosaics. "That's the Holy Spirit," a man replied, and I stopped to look at them more closely as they seemed to depict what I was feeling. Just what exactly was going on? Would I like the answer? Another time I was sitting in Saint George's and a man came running in. Saint George's is what you would call high Anglican Church of Ireland – some would say closest to the Catholic Church after the Reformation, or as one person said to me, "Them boys think they are Catholics."

"Excuse me," the man said, "what's that table sitting at the front?"

"You mean the altar," I said.

"They are talking about doing that in the Catholic churches. What kind of church is this? They have candles as well?" he asked, confused.

"Well, I can tell you that it's where Holy Communion takes place," I said. "It's what you would call high church."

"But if the Catholic churches put the altar there in their churches as well, what's the difference? What's all the fuss about?" he said.

"I'm trying to work out the same thing," I said, as he huffed and puffed out the door exasperated.

Chapter 3: Four Years into the Process

What became clear after a period of time was the physical effect the process was having on me. I didn't really believe in God, was still annoyed with organised religion, enjoyed singing but wasn't convinced by everything else. My intellectual mind was trying to figure something out but my inner essence seemed to be following another path. In particular, I noticed that friends I met had the same petty worries or annoyances as years earlier. Every time I saw them, they were complaining about the same things, were worried about the same issues, whereas my mind was elsewhere thinking about how beautiful the sky was, how fresh the wind was and how clear the birdsong – the birds just seemed so happy! The hamster-wheel worries of my mind had disappeared, and it grew amazingly crystal clear and calm; able to deal with anything life threw at me.

I felt better and better; the physical exhaustion in my job a distant memory. I kept saying I was in transition but didn't really know what I was transitioning into. I did know, however, that my heart involuntarily lifted at the thought of going to church. I loved the opportunity to sing if it came along, and my voice got better – once in a service I felt as if honey was trickling down my throat.

At a service in Taughmonagh four years in I was momentarily annoyed that my camera wouldn't work, as I was still pretending to myself that this was just an art project. I soon realised, however, that it was much more than that and the photos didn't matter as much as I'd originally thought. Damn, I thought, I'm actually starting to like this! Many times upon talking to congregants they would invite me to join their church when I'd completed my project. "Do come and join us when you're finished," they said. "Have you found a home yet?" Which brought me to a difficult question: when would I be finished? I had by that time started to tell people that I was visiting every church in Belfast, but at some point that would come to an end. How would I feel then? Would I survive it? Burst into flames? Would I stop going?

It took two years for me not to get annoyed when I heard "God", which might be useful to know for anyone who feels the same as I did or someone who is trying to connect with a person at the beginning of their faith journey. Blind obedience just wasn't in my character. Then one day I could hear the word "God" without wincing. Still not sure what I believed, I conceded that even with my doubting, questioning mind something had physically happened to me. A shift had occurred. It felt that while my head was trying to work out what it was all about intellectually, my spirit was going through some sort of cleansing process, it seemed to be washing away knots of hardness from my inner life on a subtle level. I was a changed person. It was like I was being cleaned from the inside out on a very deep level. Everything became more beautiful.

In talking to someone heavily involved with New Age seeking about what I was doing and the effect it had on me, they were appalled at the thought of it because they had been brought up in one of our dominant religious traditions and had rarely taken a step over the threshold of another. All local religious traditions were seen as a line never to be crossed; the historical burden too much to move through emotionally. I can understand how that position came about and the challenges potential congregations and churches face in trying to overcome it – there is very deep intergenerational trauma in Northern Ireland.

There is also some amazingly well-educated clergy around who in some cases would be very useful to New Age seekers, but it seems the two shall never meet, which is a great pity. I had an idea once of running a blind-date evening between clergy and the general public. They would get to ask each other questions and connect potential seekers with different churches. The public could check out the clergy before deciding if they wanted to try out their congregation. Maybe one day I will do it. It sometimes seems like people are too constrained in their structures and hierarchy and people lack the casual opportunities to connect with clergy in an informal, respectful questioning way.

I could see the importance that some churches have in building community and fellowship in areas; they look after each other, particularly within the elderly population that exists. With no children of my own it was joyful just to see children on a Sunday morning, something that many parents looking for a child-free break might find surprising.

Chapter 4: Update your Sectarianism

One day someone's comment, "My granny always said Presbyterians were very dour people," was the statement I found myself discussing, and it occurred to me that many people in Northern Ireland carry around prejudices or perspectives handed down from their grandparents and never questioned. Well, I'd found whole Presbyterian churches that were bouncing with activity and joy. Here was a well-educated, well-travelled contemporary Belfastian involved in development work holding an image of an entire section of people that was developed over a hundred years ago and never changed or challenged, maybe only whispered or joked about, and for many it was acceptable to say such a thing.

I overheard a tour guide say she liked to keep people in a room and tell them everything her father, an IRA man, used to say about Protestants. She also said she went to a Protestant service for Communion once – "Sure, no one would know who I was," she said, but thought Protestants very stingy as they only had white bread and not the real host, referring to the circular communion wafers distributed in Catholic churches. Intergenerational ignorance unchecked and given greater weight when repeated to international visitors.

A couple from the south of Ireland who were coming to Belfast to start a personal development business with a spiritual dimension said, "You know the way nobody goes to church anymore?" I replied that they were wrong, "You're in Northern Ireland now – what about the Presbyterians, Methodists, Brethren, Pentecostals?" "Oh, yes, my mum told me about the Presbyterians," was the reply as she rolled her eyes. Once again someone reaching into the family memories of what another denomination was like in another age; having little inclination or opportunity to discover for themselves the truth or falsehoods behind the comments from years past and simply thinking it was fine not to bother; taking on learned behaviours from previous generations when the current situation is very different; and coming up against the barrier of invisible, or sometimes visible, intergenerational militarisation that was necessary or not at some point or another and is now stuck behind a crust of trauma.

How do I know all this? Because that person was me. I remember someone asking me casually in my forties what was a non-subscribing Presbyterian. I remember replying that it was something to do with money, because I'd asked a school friend during the Troubles who had been brought up in the faith and that was the reply I got. The unofficial explanation that I found helpful, for those of you interested, was that ministers, elders, students and licentiates are not required to subscribe or sign adherence to the Westminster Confession of Faith. They believe that the Scriptures, Old and New Testament, are the rule of Christian faith and believe in the right of private judgement with each person having personal responsibility to read the Scriptures and in a prayerful communion with God come to an understanding of what they have read. It means that not everybody believes exactly the same thing, and that faith is a deeply personal matter between each individual and God.

I felt reluctant to talk about what I was doing, knowing I would have to cope with the verbal barrage of abuse I expected to get. (Just to make this clear: in my mind it would be from the secular community, not the clergy and congregations. After all, that is the viewpoint I used to have myself.) But I became bolder in telling people what I was up to and enjoyed discussing any aspect they were interested in. "Is it true what they say about ..." became a favourite question.

One person asked me if I sent a letter before visiting a church – Clonard Unity Pilgrims do this, and it made me smile. "No, I just wear a nice coat and turn up," was my reply. Even that answer was telling. The Unity Pilgrims are a group of ordinary Catholics at Clonard Monastery off the Falls Road in west Belfast, who, after an early Mass each Sunday, visit Protestant churches to worship with them. They were started by Father Gerry Reynolds (now deceased), a Redemptorist priest, in 1994. When I found out about them and what they do I was so surprised and pleased.

A colleague who was a participant on a development programme once told me they were tasked to do something with another religion that was unusual and perhaps outside their comfort zone. Thinking they had dealt with all their emotional triggers, a Protestant policeman and my colleague decided to attend a Catholic Mass with one of the Catholic participants on the programme. Both turned up in an outfit suitable for a wedding, to which the Catholic participant said, "Spot the Protestant!" and burst into laughter.

Dress codes tend to be different in each church, with Roman Catholic chapels more casual, except in middle-class areas. Sunday best can mean very different things, but there is a perception among many that dress is important. Noticing that hat wearing was very popular in certain churches I at times asked if it was a requisite only to be told by some elderly ladies, "Oh, no, dear, we just like the fashion," and "We don't get many opportunities to dress up these days, so we like to make an effort." Once I noticed lots of beautiful hats and pointed to some spare berets on a cloakroom hanger and asked if I should wear one. I was instead offered a piece of handmade lace to place on my head, which is probably the closest thing I've ever had to wearing a veil. The spiritual energy in that particular church was heightened, so I felt it was worth it.

How these customs and man-made rules came about I'm not entirely sure, but what is the deeper issue? Which man made the rules? Why not just, come as you are? People in Protestant churches do tend to dress up more doing their best or Sunday best in different measure. But there is a generational difference in many churches with smart casual being very popular. In working-class areas of Belfast the men tend to wear suits while the younger men avoid eye contact. To me, perhaps it gives an indication of how comfortable they feel in a social setting with a woman they don't know. In Catholic working class services men rarely wear suits to Mass unless they are politicians.

Going to church on one side of a peace line and then a church on the other side the next week, I was struck by the vast difference in church and chapel services. You can walk into a service in Saint Matthew's in the majority Catholic Short Strand and worship with an inner-city working-class congregation who have experienced much suffering intergenerationally. In fact, I would recommend it to anybody in the-Troubles-were-nothing-to-do-with-my-family's-position-and-never-affected-us brigade. Just go and feel what decades of inequality have resulted in. See if you care enough to do anything about it. Contemplate the net they've put up to stop paint being thrown over houses on the interface. Think about the flashpoint that has been around there for over a hundred years.

After visiting Saint Matthew's in Short Strand, an area with a population of around three thousand people and about three hundred people going to regular Mass, I wondered what would happen if the congregation went to Westbourne Presbyterian, Reverend Mervyn Gibson's church, on the Newtownards Road, just around the corner, where a service is like a concert with a few prayers and a sermon thrown in. But as he is the grand chaplain of the Orange Order this seems highly unlikely. I've heard him preach on a number of occasions: once at Stormont for the anniversary of the Ulster Covenant, where I thought he was quite measured, and on another occasion when his church was having repairs and the congregation gathered in a recently renovated primary school on Templemore Avenue – now the East Belfast Network Centre. This occasion was a Christmas family service – you could feel how the change of location had galvanised the congregation – and he spoke about walking around an English garden centre looking for signs of Christmas and eventually finding a few nativity scenes thrown in boxes at the feet of Santa; a taste of how many people see Christmas – thrown at the bottom of commercialisation.

On that occasion I was introduced to his wife (which sometimes happens in working-class churches), and we had a nice talk about what I was doing. She asked me what type of services I preferred. We had a good chat about some of the variety that there is on offer. After that particular service I walked on Templemore Avenue. A couple of teenagers were sitting outside in their pyjamas speaking on their mobiles. I met a boy in the newsagents who I knew from art interventions around the area. He had drawn a laughing man with a machine gun shooting another man. On a Sunday morning he was looking for sweets. To the wider world he would be perceived as Protestant, but as far as I could work out, he had never set foot in a church for a service.

Another newly branded church that has taken over a Baptist building on the Newtownards Road seemed contemporary and looked interior designed; skyping in its minister from Thailand during the service with high-energy music and voices clear. But on second thoughts I felt it offered the same as Westbourne Presbyterian just packaged differently. Is it all just about branding?

Strangely, I found that I was never bored, which quite honestly surprised me. What if all the church walls dissolved on a Sunday morning and everyone across the city could see what was going on? What indeed!

At church, if anyone asked me who I was, we got into a chat. "What a lovely thing to do," was often a reply and, "When are you bringing out the book?" another. Only once in a gospel hall was a woman so dumbstruck by what I was doing that she couldn't speak and simply stared at me, walking away backwards, horrified by what she'd just heard. At a Baptist church, a young pastor's wife with her baby didn't really know what to say when I told her I felt I belonged everywhere. She just lifted her baby and went for tea. When I told a minister in north Belfast what I was doing, he asked was I sure that someone wouldn't just think, "What is that stupid woman doing, wasting her time?" It made me ponder on the nature of freedom.

I thought of the clergy and laypeople in different buildings or churches – whatever form they take – throughout the city, how those structures came about and what, if any, common thread they had. I started to see the city in a different light and felt comforted that there were so many people on a daily and weekly basis reaching out to something of a spiritual nature. I was beginning to see Belfast as a city of light, a light that has been hidden in plain sight.

The entwining of religion and Northern Ireland's violent past brings great challenges to people if they want to first recognise and then update their sectarianism. Many people hold perspectives and grudges that have been handed down through their families for generations; perspectives developed in different eras perhaps, based on real incidents and genuine fears and experiences. Trauma is rife in the city, and the result is that many point to past oppression rather than the contemporary reality for many religious denominations. There is much discussion about Protestants and Catholics in Northern Ireland going back hundreds of years and yet with a shift in religious observance, are these divisions still so relevant?

A member of the Roman Catholic community might have joined the IRA or one of its offshoots for any number of reasons, but are they still a practicing church-attending Catholic? Or have they gone a la carte? The UFF, UVF, UDA sprung from Protestants, but how many are practicing church-attending Protestants?

"My dad says religion's boring," said the boys I encountered on the Newtownards Road. They talked of their excitement of being in the East Belfast Protestant Boys marching band, yet when I said to them that Protestantism is a religion, they said, "No, it's not," and duly hummed "The Sash" while marching up and down, playing imaginary drumsticks, saying that is what Protestantism is.

I related this story once at the West Belfast Festival when Dan Gordon was showing the documentary on the making of his play about bandsmen. A Bandsman was at the talk. He shrugged it off and said, "Yes, well, there was a movement to try and link the bands back to the Protestant religion they claim to glorify." A Methodist minister told me she would often get a phone call from people wanting to join the Orange Order because Orangemen are supposed to be part of a church congregation but she refuses to add their names to her congregation because she knows she'll never see them. There are of course many who belong to the Orange Order who do have a faith but not all. Part of the difficult lens we view religion through in Northern Ireland comes from our society's traumatised past relating to militarism and paramilitarism.

It's obvious in attending services that some Protestant congregations have had the economic benefits of opportunity built up over generations, while in other churches it's obvious that whole congregations have been blocked from the same opportunities until more recently. This is rarely discussed but is a real and difficult issue to broach, which is often dismissed by the better off.

There are studies and research into a subject area that could be a book in itself, but for the purposes of this book I think it's important to comprehend some basics about trauma as I understand them. The brain has synapses that fire information to each other. When someone is traumatised, their brain can stop firing these synapses to make new thoughts, and instead the same thoughts fire over and over again, keeping the traumatised person with the same thought patterns, totally unable to have new thoughts.

Art is one way to soften these synapses and help people have new thoughts. As attitudes soften with time, moving away from the worst of the violence, we can only hope that people find safer spaces to update their perspectives. On more than one occasion I was listening to people talk shyly about a post-Protestant–post-Catholic society, showing an awareness that old labels are becoming less relevant. We can only hope. After all, it's been five hundred years since the Reformation.

Part of the difficulty we experience in Northern Ireland is that many of our leaders rely on this trauma existing, and are adept at fear mongering especially at election times – some of them are traumatised themselves, and then we have a civil service that is used to dealing with the fallout of the trauma which I would also suggest belong to the traumatized government. Among all this there is an expectation to come up with new ideas on how to deal with it, yet these structures were built during a time of conflict and an absence of risk in mind. I've been in meetings with organisations and civil servants delivering programmes to those keeping the peace, and I have been continuously blocked, laughed at and dismissed as there is no mechanism or thought processes available to contemplate something different – or if there is it challenges the person's position in the traumatised structure and so they don't want to support it. After all, they need to keep paying their mortgage.

In 2018, after Culture Night, an annual Belfast city centre event that animates the streets and cultural institutions, I travelled home on the Glider the new rapid transport system that travels across town. It was packed with lots of teenagers talking about how much they love Culture Night. One young guy, probably seventeenish, is slightly drunk. He tells the gathered passengers, "See all this Protestant–Catholic stuff, that's over. We are Northern Ireland and that's the way it is. I'm a Christian, that's what's important." Someone on the bus asked if he wanted to get off at Stormont.

I would never stop someone seeking justice and truth, but, as I walked around a Relatives for Justice exhibition at Féile an Phobail, all I could think of was – how are these relatives finding healing? How can we stop the process of transferring trauma from one generation to another? Is that something we can start while relatives are still lobbying for justice, considering that justice itself doesn't bring healing?

There was an installation in the corridors of Saint Mary's University College, Belfast – a pair of shoes belonging to people from west Belfast who had died during the Troubles. Each set of shoes had a label attached written by family members with details of their owner. I imagined them all in a church as an exhibit for quiet contemplation. I mentioned this to the late Reverend Margaret Ferguson of East Belfast Mission. "I would take the shoes and pray with them," said Margaret, "and invite the families." Would this spiritual act help healing?

I once went to a retreat run by Miranda Macpherson, an Australian spiritual leader based in America, who had set up an interfaith seminary in England. The core lessons I learned from the experience were around her comments on anger being based on hurt, and that when hurt is transmuted it becomes wisdom. Those words resonated with me strongly as after all my years in cross-community work I felt angry, angry at the structures, angry at the hurt, angry with the world, deep in the pit of my stomach. It was a physical manifestation of absorbing so much of other people's trauma. It disappeared somewhere about two years in to my church visiting. But there are still many in Northern Ireland who are still very angry.

In 2016, one hundred years after the Easter Rising, some have been able to transmute their hurt while others hold onto it like a trophy; eager to parade it through our towns and villages, sometimes offering it to anyone of a different religion rather than open-hearted love. Hopefully the Orange Order have passed their more difficult years, but anger still prevails. There are always those on the margins ready to take advantage of any power vacuums. Many are caught up in a structure and left in a dissolute state but, Miranda says, "Pain becomes part of our wisdom body. We just have to present undefended and open-hearted and healing happens."

I, like many others in Northern Ireland, have experienced people guessing my religion and then launching a personal attack because of it. It comes because we're all wounded, but unless you've processed this it can be quite shocking and even dangerous. Growing up, I learned ways to hide my religion out of real fear and the need for

24

security. As an adult working in all areas of Belfast, I became deft at sidestepping the issue, not revealing the religion I was born into, covering my tracks.

Maybe we should focus on finding a way to acknowledge each other's pain and listen? It's taken me years to feel comfortable in places that would have been dangerous for me when I was growing up, but I'm aware that not everyone is in the same place as me and instead they transfer their own position of trauma onto the generations that follow them.

I accept and acknowledge that the religious communities in Northern Ireland have had different opportunities and these opportunities have resulted in conflict. But now that we are post-conflict, well, trying desperately to be, what has been the impact on the spirit of those who remain? The one common thing the Veteran's for Peace say about war/ conflict is that when it's over we all have to deal with who is still alive.

I once heard Reverend Norman Hamilton say that he was looking into research on people who have suffered the violent death of a family member and seek justice. The research suggested that after loved ones found out who did it, they didn't feel any better and wondered why. Is it because it's a different process? Going up to an event in the West Belfast festival for family members who were affected by Troubles deaths, I was disappointed to find it was postponed, as the lawyer who had organized it felt the customers who would come, and yes that was the word given to me, customers would be similar to another event that was happening. I slipped into the other event and looked and listened. The audience was being encouraged down a legal route for political and personal advantage which is their right. Their visible suffering was acknowledged but there was no mention of personal healing. I heard at a Hanna's House Conference in Dublin I heard Dawn Purvis, the ex-PUP MLA, speaking eloquently about the people around her, including friends and parents, who had died during the Troubles. She said, "People would just like to know what happened."

At another event during the Féile an Phobail, where the Police ombudsman Dr Michael Maguire was delivering a talk before his retirement a man in the audience asked what someone would get out of telling a person's family member the circumstances of their relatives death, it seemed to me that the man in question had forgotten more than one of his cultural religions teachings, that of love and forgiveness and the release from being heavily burdened.

Chapter 5: Just How Many Churches Are There?

I never stopped to count how many churches there were in Belfast – I think I was afraid of the answer, and what exactly would the answer represent anyway? I didn't want that feeling of dread after seeing a long list; seeing years of church attendance stretching out in front of me and turning me into some sort of endless sitting, standing, praying automat. I still couldn't believe I was actually doing what I was doing, but one day I decided to see if I could find a list – surely there was a list somewhere – and I headed to Holywood Arches Library. Always shy of saying what I was doing outside a church environment, as sometimes people's eyes glazed over or I got a wary look in case I started preaching or handing out tracts, I found myself starting the conversation with, "I'm not religious but …". I told the librarian I was attending a service in every church in Belfast and asked, "Is there a list anywhere locating every church in Belfast?"

The librarian stopped in her tracks and thought for a while. "There is a book about the, Clergymen of Belfast in Belfast Central Library."

"What about clergywomen?" I asked.

"Oh, there's not too many of them around," a fellow librarian replied.

"Oh, but there are," was my reply.

It has been a delightful surprise to see just how many clergywomen are now serving in the churches in Belfast. Informally I've been told that churches that include women in their clergy have avoided closing because not enough men are having religious callings any more. I heard Father Martin Magill say, "God's still calling but people do not seem to be listening," or did he mean men weren't listening?

I often found on my rounds that clergywomen can bring a different perspective to the proceedings, using scripture as poetry and delivering sermons with acute finesse. But are the institutions themselves too male? Are some clergywomen suffering a similar fate to when women took roles in business, dressed more like men and downplayed their feminine nature taking on male characteristics? Are

27

they tolerated because they are status quo supporters? Where is the divine feminine?

One female cleric told me that during one of her lectures at theology college a lecturer said, "God is calling men. They are not listening, so he has to call women." Not surprisingly the comment made her jump and interesting discussions followed.

I went to Belfast Central Library, explaining again what I was doing. The young man I asked paused for a deep breath, "Let me see." He appeared back with a book on clergymen of Belfast and another on street businesses to include churches. "It would be much easier if there was just one church," the young man said as he searched the computer.

"But it's Belfast – that's partly what all the fuss is about," was my reply.

After sitting down with my books at the other end of the library, the young man came running to me with some printouts. "Methodist churches in Belfast, don't forget about these," he said.

Bet you he's from Methodist stock, I thought.

Off I went with an incomplete list knowing that many churches I'd already visited weren't in any of the listings I'd found – interesting that there isn't one definitive list considering Belfast's historic relationship with religion. A surprise to some is that new churches are popping up all the time. Each time I think I've covered a complete area I'll find a new church or be told of yet another church starting.

One such church was in Clarawood estate, east Belfast. I discovered it by finding a poly pocket attached to a gate with an A4 sheet inside: "Church, 11 a.m. Sunday" was typed on it. On entering I found a guitarist, a pastor and two congregants. A highly energetic service proceeded and at one point they quoted that to give is to receive, and thirty per cent of your salary is good enough. They were the only church I found to have basic leaflets and notes on coming into Christianity and what to expect. On talking with them afterwards I found out that they came from mid-Ulster and wanted to plant a church. Not really knowing Belfast, they looked around for somewhere they felt wasn't currently serviced, and they had plans to reach out around the estate. As I left, I saw one desolate elderly man and his dog grimace in the morning light. I wished them well, thinking that the man might benefit from a little love and light. Six months later I came back to see what had happened and found that the church had gone.

After believing I'd attended all the churches in Tullycarnet, one Sunday I noticed a flag outside a community centre: "East Point Church". The following week I attended. Only eight months after it had started in a sports hall, the service was ninety per cent full, intergenerational and bouncing with energy and grace.

It seems that there is always a church waiting to flourish somewhere in the wings. Ten years into the process I took some time to research if there were any churches I missed only to find another thirty-one, no doubt more have continued to pop up. Belfast is far from a secular wasteland.

Chapter 6: The Rhythms of the Seasons

I noticed a redundant liturgy calendar on the stairs of The National, a cafe bar in the Cathedral Quarter in Belfast. Although I was wondering what church it once hung in and what became of the people who used to look at it, I understood that others are disconnected from any awareness of church in contemporary Belfast. This calendar was discarded like many discard any connection with organised religion and was reduced to only being glanced at as people made their way to the bar or the loo.

However, one of the interesting results of regular church attendance is the connection or reconnection to the seasons. I became more aware of a wider connection of the passing months of the year with the liturgy. Slipping back into the artistic community allowed me to see things differently too. Once when watching a piece of performance art by Elvira Santamaria in Catalyst Arts Gallery, Elvira stood in quiet contemplation, deep in the moment of her art piece. In the semi-darkness I saw a light emanating from her being. What on earth was this? Later, I came across spiritual light. I contemplated if that was what I saw.

One Sunday I felt I was stepping back in time when I went out on a cold, dark winter morning, arriving at Saint Malachy's Catholic Church in the Markets area of inner-city Belfast. The church was originally to be a cathedral, but when the famine hit Ireland the building work stopped. Newly renovated with decorative plastered high ceilings and a glittery glow, it was a marked contrast to the dull, grey Belfast winter's day outside.

Apparently the peal from the church bell once interfered with the distilling process of a local distillery and so it was muffled, but on this morning I was aware of just how spectacular the event of churchgoing must have been when church was all the entertainment there was, when the local church was the largest, most spectacular building a person ever found themselves in. It would have been community building, fellowship and friendship cementing. The communal worship the weekly entertainment; offering connection to everyone and an awareness of seasonal variations: harvest, Christmas, Easter, Pentecost, the gathering and acts of worship connecting people's spiritual selves. I knew that so many people are now disconnected from that awareness, with instant twenty-four-hour entertainment and the bright colours of the flashing TVs, computer and phone screens everywhere, pulling our inner life to outer distraction, making day-to-day reality much flatter and more boring with little time for thoughts of transcendence or spirit.

Is this why our suicide rate is so high? Many of our young people, don't have anything to strive for other than being a consumer in a world with little opportunity of working to afford and being able to consume; thinking instead that if only they could satisfy the next desire, everything would be well. If only they could be kept entertained, all would be well. If only they looked a certain way, all would be okay. Consumerism perhaps makes them feel whole, and the next foreign holiday fulfilled – the modern disease of busyness and distraction, but what of the world of the spirit – where does it dwell?

Christmas feels different. As I drive to a service on Christmas Eve, passing all the open churches, it reinforces again just how much living spirituality exists in the city of Belfast. Christmas congregations tend to be different too. Church going can be a once-a-year event, nostalgia brings them out, and as a result churches are full of people vibrating at a different level. They are wanted but there's no doubt it feels different to be among them. What I mean is, their spiritual practice is such that you can feel it on entering the church. I can go to a church during the year and on entering feel the presence of a rarefied spirit; a communal energy developed I think by the people present who have been practising their spirituality. As the service progresses, usually the feelings are amplified, but when a church is filled with non-regular churchgoers there is a different feeling in the building.

Vibrating at a different level in a large group has the effect of blunting the ecstatic energy. The children brought once a year are distracted, fidgeting in their seats, sometimes running up and down the aisles. All are very much welcomed with open arms but often there's a dullness in their eyes. Some congregants look like they've been brought under duress, asking what's it all about – if they're thinking at all.

After a while I found that the only place I loved to be in large groups was in a church congregation. I met Father Gerry Reynolds in Belfast City Council's Lord Mayor's Parlour at the launch of the 4 Corners Festival in 2015. We talked about what I was doing. As we shook hands, I felt some sort of electric connection between us.

"Tell me this," he said, "isn't there no better feeling than collective worship with a congregation?"

"No, there isn't," I replied. Never did I think this would have been my reply.

You do wonder – when you go to a service on one side of the city and see two grown-ups dressed as sheep delivering the nativity story, as in Christian Fellowship Church in Belmont, then travel to the other side of the city and hear the voices of Schola Cantorum at Saint Peter's Catholic Cathedral, followed by more traditional singing and praying – just how this difference has come about. How did this wide interpretation of spiritual practice happen in one city? Man-made rules? What has been left behind, after all these fallouts and break-ups, of different denominations to an ancient spiritual pulse that many people don't believe exists.

After about three years of church attendance the dark, depressing days of January and February have become a distant memory. It was always the most difficult time of year for me, as it is for many in Northern Ireland, with dark skies and dreary weather, but that stir-crazy feeling at the end of the winter has gone. The dark evenings and seasonal weather of Ireland no longer affect me negatively. I no longer look for a winter holiday and other escapism to get me through. Now, as I sit writing this in Belfast, a drizzly morning has made way for a windy afternoon, and although the shift of the winter solstice has occurred, spring still seems far away. For many years this would have filled me with a sadness and unsettled daily existence; counting the days until the weather broke and the snowdrops came, begging for a trip to Barcelona for some heat and light. Now the dark evenings and wet days never cause me a second thought. It's as if there is a buffer of light between my inner self and the outer world that keeps humming joyfully and bringing contentment wherever it goes. That in itself is worth much. People around me say, "Oh, it's so dark," and I reply, "But the light is on the inside."

Congregations at this time of year can be a great source of uplifting energy. No longer with the once-a-year Christmas churchgoers among their ranks, their combined energy can be soft and inspiring. Smiling eyes abound.

The ancient Irish poets used to, as part of their training, spend the winter days in darkness creating verse and only come out at night. It is said to have developed an inner light in their internal chambers, and often when it came time for them to go back into the daytime light, they missed the darkness, as it was their time with the light. Compare this to the human race now: distracted, disconnected, aggressive, sometimes suicidal, reaching for distraction and stimulants to get them by, unaware or uninterested in their human beingness and the internal riches of their inner core. What if those poets had had a mobile phone?

Rev. Grace Clunie of the Centre for Celtic Spirituality in Navan asked me how I thought this had happened – how did the light occur? I can only say that the light wasn't what I was seeking and I often tried to walk away from it. What I think has happened to me is that by reconnecting with my artistic practice I've reconnected to my inner essence, the essential nature I'd developed at an earlier age. When I stopped working in the traumatised structures that helped people, I rediscovered my creative joy and slowly the light reappeared. Church attendance made it brighter, and each time I go it seems to get recharged in a slightly different way depending on the people in the church and the depth of their own spirits and the soul energy of a place.

For Easter week in 2018 I decided to try and go deeper into my church service experience. Finding myself in the city centre on Ash Wednesday, I noticed a lunchtime service giving ashes at Saint George's Church of Ireland. As schoolchildren during the Troubles we wondered why people walked around with such an obvious sign of their religion when people were being shot dead in the street for less.

A small congregation arrived and the minister, using his finger, put a spot of ashes into the middle of my forehead where the Hindu bindi rests, or other people believe the inner eye to be located. He said something like, "We come from ashes. We return to ashes."

I cycled home afterwards and luckily had little to do that afternoon as I felt like the whole world was travelling through my head – a sort of giant cosmic stream focused on the spot where the ashes were given, as if I was connected to some giant cosmic wheel.

On Ash Wednesday 2019 I attended the 10 a.m. service at Saint Patrick's Catholic Church and the local primary-school children were in attendance. When giving the ashes the nun said something like, "Repent of your sins and adhere to the gospel." Although I felt very connected all day, it was quite a different experience than that of Saint George's. It felt like I was being pushed down rather than connected up spiritually

On Easter Sunday 2018 I woke predawn with an unknown brightness and followed the moon from Strangford to Inch Abbey for the dawn service. Now in ruins, it was a Cistercian abbey; the first monastery established on the northern banks of the Quoile River in AD 800, and known as Inis Crumhscraigh. The Very Reverend Henry Hull, Dean of Down, said, "It was a pity that such stones would be alone on Easter Sunday."

Slowly people gathered, and crows squawked as dawn arrived. The assembled eighty or so stood in a semicircle among the ruins while a Communion service took place. Someone talked about the year they'd been stopped by the police as they were driving so slowly to get to Inch. The officers must have thought he was under the influence of alcohol but he said, "No, officer, I'm going to the dawn service at Inch Abbey." Everyone laughed.

The clergy from various denominations arrived, some with capes, and someone commented, "It's all very *Game of Thrones*," in the half-light. There was joviality and camaraderie, and the congregation walked over to a nearby church hall where bacon butties and tea were a welcome refreshment served to the gathering crowds. An amazing experience. As it was still early, I thought I would go to Saul where Saint Patrick's first church was built and walk up to see his statue high on the hill. The beautiful County Down drumlins were glowing in all their Easter freshness. I remembered all the years of travelling into Downpatrick on the school bus during the Troubles and delighted in the joy that this generation growing up didn't have the same experience. Still early, I caught a packed Saint Patricks Catholic

Church Saul for its Easter service. As it was busy I walked up to the front of the chapel where there were still seats. The flowers were beautiful and, of course, included the Easter lily. The priest talked about the reality of Christ's crucifixion and resurrection and then about worldly things and mindfulness that are simply feel-good factors but lack core teaching. During the collection I was passed over, and then I realised that perhaps I was sitting in some specially reserved seats for extraordinary ministers of the Eucharist as the two other people on my pew got up to give Communion. As is normal in Catholic churches, no one spoke to me, but I looked at all the children in their Easter outfits wanting to go home and enjoy their Easter eggs. I wondered whether they might play with the Church of Ireland kids over the hill in another church. What would Saint Patrick think of it all?

Chapter 7: Saint Patrick's Day

The ways you can celebrate Saint Patrick's Day in Northern Ireland, away from the drinks' promotions and parades, is as large and varied as the stories around the saint himself. I've had some interesting experiences over the years, but discussion around whether Saint Patrick was Protestant or Catholic are still ongoing with much misinformation and some from the Protestant tradition distancing themselves from the celebrations entirely. Nevertheless, I've marvelled at hearing Saint Patrick's prayer sang by the choir in Clonard Monastery, and been given a bookmark with the prayer and a Celtic cross on it in Saint Donard's Church of Ireland in east Belfast. In the service in Down Cathedral in 2017 St Patrick's prayer was sang in the last hymn, like an extra verse, leading to such an overwhelming feeling of light that I could hardly stand up. I've experienced a minister wrapped in a green feather boa, wearing a "kiss me I'm Irish" tie and a leprechaun hat giving a sermon in Saint Donard's Church of Ireland, only to think that if other denominations did that the cleric would be escorted off the premises!

Irish dancers are lovely to see in church on St Patrick's Day, and in one Irish language service I attended in Downpatrick they gave out some robustly blessed shamrock, which lasted well beyond everyone else's. At that particular Irish language service I saw someone who was surprised to see me there. She said under her breath, "I'm noticing all the Sinn Féin people are here for the service but not one of them went up for Communion," whatever that was supposed to mean.

To the small early Mass congregation in Clonard Monastery a few years ago, the priest said it was important for everyone to remember that throughout the ages religious observance had gone up and down in popularity, and that at the moment we were just experiencing a down period, but that the congregants gathered that day were some of those who would hold the light of faith. I looked around the congregation and saw Mary Hughes and her daughter Susan. Mary, now deceased, was a wonderful woman who was a participant on a women's development programme I ran many years ago. Wise in an ancient way, she told me once that the only way she got through some times in her life was to go to the early Mass at Clonard Monastery every day. I had tweeted a picture of the altar to a friend and told her where I was. She got confused about the location and went to Saint Peter's Cathedral on the Falls Road instead. At least it was a new experience for her!

So far, my favourite service to attend for Saint Patrick's Day is Saul, just outside Downpatrick, and the location of Saint Patrick's first church. The small church building is within the Down and Dromore Diocese of the Church of Ireland and the Bishop of Down and Dromore leads the pilgrimage that attracts people from all over the world. As it's usually overflowing with pilgrims, you can receive Communion outside, deep in the drumlin-filled landscape. Afterwards, a pilgrimage walk to Downpatrick is in order, with people taking turns to carry the cross at the front. Only a two-mile walk, but lovely to be walking through the County Down drumlins with that wonderful fresh-air feeling. The walk itself started many years ago – there is a wonderful clip of it on the British Film Institute's website from 1959. There you cannot help but notice the lack of women clergy. The pilgrimage stopped for a number of years during the Troubles only to be reinstated in more recent times, and has been growing in popularity, remaining my favourite thing to do on Saint Patrick's Day.

Once in Downpatrick the crowd walks up the hill to the cathedral. Walking around the corner into the packed cathedral to music playing is quite a thrilling feeling. Free Irish stew and apple tart is offered afterwards in a marquee on the grounds. With all the people milling around it's the only time you get a feeling for what it must have felt like in the times when it was one of the most popular pilgrimage sites in Ireland.

One year it was surreal to see the Archbishop of Canterbury Justin Welby standing outside the front door of the Cathedral giving blessings to people as they patiently queued. He'd given a brilliant sermon on how Downpatrick preceded anything that happened in Lambeth Palace, where he leads the Church of England. I watched a bewildered young woman and her dad; she had an Irish tricolour painted on her face among a sea of Church of Ireland pilgrims unaware of the politics of what she was doing. She was welcome none the less.

The same year that Justin Welby was in Downpatrick for Saint Patrick's Day, he was at the Waterfront in Belfast on the same evening for Saint Patricks Peace Party a cross-community gathering of young people and invited clergy. Somehow an invitation came to me, or I saw the invite somewhere, and my husband and I trooped down to watch a very confident Jasper Rutherford European Director of Christ in Youth interview the archbishop and stand at one point with his hand on his back to pray for him. The interview included a talk with Nichola Mallon, SDLP, who was Lord Mayor of Belfast at the time. She spoke of her faith and how everyone thought that when she went to university in Dublin, she would ditch it, yet she continued to be an extraordinary minister of the Eucharist. The group walked (it was important it wasn't labelled a parade) to the city hall, past young people drinking outside a club and snogging at the side of a police Land Rover. Nichola Mallon said a prayer, as did a number of young people and then the archbishop. We were then asked to hold hands and pray into the night sky for Belfast. There was a lovely uplifting feeling and just at the end a wave of sweet energy flowed. I couldn't help but note that in my teenage years it was more likely that I would have been the one doing the snogging than the praying but thought just how much better off these young participants were.

The graveyard in the grounds of the cathedral is where Saint Patrick is supposed to be buried along with Saint Brigid and Saint Colmcille. As a teenager going to school nearby, I used to sit in the cathedral and draw. With its vaulted ceilings and symmetrical light fittings, it was quite a challenge to do any realistic drawings. It was also the place we used to have our school Christmas carol services. In the grounds is the grave of the husband of my primary-seven teacher and father of my best friend at primary school, shot dead on the streets of Downpatrick. Such is the nature of the layers of history and trauma flowing along our meandering past.

In 2017 Bishop Harold Millar (now retired) said to the gathered congregation, "It's about time in Northern Ireland that we all wised up. Saint Patrick was here long before Protestants and Catholics." The congregation nodded their heads but I couldn't see what James

Brokenshire, the secretary of state for Northern Ireland at the time, was doing from where I was sitting. I've heard Bishop Harold say on other occasions that the days of churches telling you what to do are over, but they can still help.

I stopped going into Belfast city centre for Saint Patrick's Day many years ago; bored with the division and potential for trouble. But in 2014 artist Breandán Clarke asked me to join an international group on a European programme. Breandán was working with North Belfast Interface Network and was key in the *Draw Down the Walls* project with the Golden Thread Gallery. A graduate of Belfast School of Art, Breandán had went into community work. We first connected online when he asked who in Belfast wanted to draw down the walls, referring to over one hundred interface walls erected with emergency powers during the Troubles – but with no emergency powers in existence to bring them down. Later we met in person and struck up a friendship. The group of people involved were from all over Europe. They were looking at history and division and were coming over for Saint Patrick's Day, interested to see how Belfast managed the parade. Somehow we were invited to the Lord Mayor's Parlour the night before.

Máirtín Ó Muilleoir, Sinn Féin, was the Lord Mayor, and he entertained the European guests. Recognising me, he asked me if I could tell the assembled group what I was up to. The next day, as we watched the parade, our group got separated when we were standing near the Albert Clock in the front row of onlookers. I watched as Máirtín stood at the front of the kilted Ulster Scots marching band, getting the young female baton twirler to teach him how to lead the band. Further on down the route he came over to the side of the crowd and spotted me, saying what a pleasant evening it had been in the parlour the night before with all the guests. He beckoned me into the procession and I reluctantly walked a hundred metres or so along the route before sneaking back into the crowd. I looked at the faces lining the route and saw working-class nationalist and republican Belfast simply ready for a day out, families that you never see out together in the city – and lots of bewildered tourists. We filmed the parade for the European project and when the footage was delivered they said they were unable to use it because of all the tri colours and it was supposed to be cross community. "But that's what it's like" I replied.

In 2018 I went back to Clonard Monastery, which was packed with the later service. I heard again Saint Patrick's prayer sang by the choir high up above and thought how different it was to the experience in Down Cathedral where I felt like I was inside the prayer, that the Holy Spirit had filled me up and I was at one with it. Walking down into the city centre, with the snow falling, I spotted a group of tourists outside the Irish shop, posing in leprechaun hats and ginger beards in front of a police Land Rover, which was in front of a Union Jack flag protest. All around young women in miniskirts were draped in Irish tricolours.

I noticed on the other side of the road two older women with the same leprechaun hats trying to get their child to take a photo of them. I went over and asked if they wanted me to take it so the children could be in the photograph as well.

"Yes, that would be great," they replied, then got in place with the Union Jacks behind them.

"Do you want me to get the police Land Rover in?" I asked.

"Yes, get the RUC in," they replied.

"You do know it's been the PSNI for quite some time now?" I said, referring to the long process of transformation that the police force had undergone since the ceasefires, including a name change.

"Ah, it's the RUC, RUC," they chanted. "This is our twelfth."

I walked over to the police Land Rover. A tourist was asking a policewoman what the Union Jack flag protest was. She explained the background to it – I zoned out, having lived through it. I walked further over to the men at the protest, the snow starting again. A man took down a flag I didn't recognise and began folding it.

"Can I ask you what flag it is?" I asked.

"It's the paratroopers, love," he replied.

Thinking that he was probably a paratrooper himself, I asked him if he had caught any of the parade.

"All those young women walking about half-naked in the cold," he said, "they would be better off home beside the fire."

"What about you?" I asked.

"That's exactly where I'm going now," he replied.

I asked another man in the protest if he saw any of the parade.

"The George Best float – I see they're claiming him now," he said.

"Who's *they*?" I asked.

"The Catholics," he replied.

"Do you know Saint Patrick was around before any religious divisions?"

"Tell them that," he replied, indicating to the people in leprechaun hats across the road.

On I walked to the Engine Room Gallery where artist Jack Pakenham was delivering a talk. Jack, now in his eighties, has an archive of paintings all the way through the Troubles. Painting daily since retirement, he processes what is going on in society in a very specific fashion. I explained that on the opening night of his exhibition I caught a young female visitor arguing with one of his paintings, trying to decipher its meaning.

"That painting is argument without end," I said, "just like Northern Ireland."

The assembled audience of art appreciators laughed or shrugged their shoulders in knowing acknowledgement.

In 2019 on Saint Patrick's Day at Clonard Monastery the priest spoke about the percentage of people who are nominal Catholics and how Saint Patrick arrived in a pre-Christian Ireland. Now it's a post-Christian Ireland, and in another couple of generations there may be very little of the faith in the country if current trends continue.

Chapter 8: Old St Pat's Chicago

On my first visit to see my long-term artistic collaborator Suellen Semekoski in Chicago, we visited the highly ornate Old Saint Patrick's Church for a lunchtime service. Old Saint Patrick's is the oldest church in Chicago and one of the few buildings that survived the Great Chicago Fire of 1871. It's a hub to the local Irish–American population, and a building with a beautiful interior of plasterwork, inspired by the *Book of Kells*, that was added around the time of the Partition of Ireland by the son of an Irishman who dug holes for a living.

"Imagine a man came here and dug holes for a living and his son was so creative he did all this beautiful work," said a parishioner.

"Now the artists are digging holes in Ireland," I replied with a slight smile.

On my second visit my return flight was delayed due to freezing weather conditions and snow. It gave me an extra day in the city, so Suellen and I decided to go to a Sunday morning service. We arrived at the last minute and just about managed to get a seat. The priest, Father Cusick, now retired, was walking down the aisle shaking people's hands and asking them where they were from. The church was packed and all very showbiz.

"Hello, how are you? We have a rose candle today – I can't even remember why," he said.

I expected someone to hit a cymbal and say "Ta-da!" not being used to a priest with an American accent.

He turned to me and when he heard I came from Belfast asked, "What are those guys doing over there? We can't have Belfast going back to violence. It's taken too long to get this far," he said.

He was talking in relation to a small pipe bomb the week before.

The service started, the priest preached and the congregation sang in full voice. Father Cusick welcomed me and someone from Florida at the front asked if I'd come for the weather! The congregation laughed as they thought of the three feet of snow outside.

It was here that I experienced an overwhelming feeling of filling up with the energy that was around me, within the people. There I was sitting in the middle of a congregation who had for generations taken its religion seriously and generated a combined energy to match. At one point the priest asked the congregation to turn around and offer each other a sign of peace. The couple behind me gave me a prayer card and asked that I bring it back to their friends in Ireland. It was a genuine and loving request and the tears welled up in my eyes as I turned back around. I could hardly stand at the end of the service, such was the feeling of being filled with light. Apparently the congregation is famous for it.

We spoke with the priest after the service and he said the only time he'd been in Ireland it had been very grey. I commented that the congregation in Old Saint Patrick's sang, unlike the majority of Catholic congregations in Northern Ireland.

"How can you ask people to come to church and not let them sing?" he said.

He talked about how every time he took a Sunday service at Old St Patrick's he felt filled with the Holy Spirit afterwards, but that it's not the building – it comes from the people. When there's such a large congregation of practicing Roman Catholics, the Holy Spirit amplifies.

When I told him about my church visits, he told me to write a book about it because he wanted to read it, and he wanted his congregation to read it to find out just what exactly is going on in Belfast.

He spoke of a young man he'd just talked to, who had been walking down a street in Chicago when the boy he was walking with was shot dead by a random shooter. Chicago has a lot of violence and these instances aren't uncommon unfortunately.

On leaving the church building I couldn't help but think back to a service I'd been to in the Short Strand area of Belfast. The difference in the congregations couldn't have been more marked: here in Chicago are the well-heeled third generation Irish Americans who benefited from getting out of Ireland and flourished under different conditions, while in the Short Strand is a congregation that stayed and tried to survive under unequal conditions during the Troubles. It has taken its toll, something you can physically see and feel. In the Short

43

Strand there isn't the same feeling of exuberant Holy Spirit. You see and feel the more immediate worries of day-to-day living. Poverty is palpable with visible health issues and this is only taking into consideration the people who are going to Mass. The community still talk of Pogroms'.

There is, however, one congregation that I felt a glow similar to that which I felt in Old Saint Patrick's, and that's the congregation in Ardoyne Sacred Heart Catholic Church, north Belfast. Its congregation glows from the inside with a devoted group of people who have experienced much of the worst of the Troubles but still seem to shine from the inside, despite it or maybe because of it. Embodied humans, perhaps?

Something I'm very well aware of is the complexity of religion in Northern Ireland, and yet when historical inequalities are so obvious, so too is the silence from those families that have benefited from the intergenerational inequality. Sometimes I think they are simply unsure what they might be able to do, or how to go about it, others simply are not interested. The simple act of visiting several church services highlights this and makes the silence even more deafening. Maybe it's time for more people to get out of their comfort zone, to go and have a look and listen, unhook themselves from old hurts, or guilt at not having any hurt, and reach out to move forward. Does fear hold us back? To survive during the Troubles, I like many other people just tried to block it out. Many I know couldn't do this. Years ago I was told this reflex was a common reaction to conflict that humans do to survive on a daily basis. Yes, I survived, and even thrived, but if your only current worry is that your children have the same social status and opportunities you had because of past inequalities, is it time to be a bit more honest and gracious – simply as a way of moving forward?

At the 4 Corners Festival in 2018, Methodist minister Reverend Harold Good developed an act of acknowledgement that I think should be taken up on a wider basis. He developed it with Reverend David Campton after trying to get people to join in on a day of reflection and realising that the things those people said back to him had nothing to do with the Troubles in that they never took up arms, never murdered anyone. At the festival the congregation took part in the following:

Act of Acknowledgement

Gracious God, in your mercy hear us as we acknowledge our failing
before you:

For those times when we elevated earthly loyalties and personal
ambition over the purposes of your Kingdom (Pause)

Lord, have mercy. **Lord, Forgive**

For those times when we have dressed personal prejudices and
worldly agendas in pious language and self-righteous indignation
(Pause)

Lord, have mercy. **Lord, Forgive**

For those times when we have been tolerant of injustice, quick to
condemn those who sin differently from us, and unwilling to
overcome evil with good (Pause)

Lord have mercy. **Lord, forgive**

For those times when we have preferred conquest to service, conflict
to peace, revenge to reconciliation, and material well-being to
spiritual satisfaction (Pause)

Lord, have mercy. **Lord, forgive**

For those times when we have been quick to divide people into us and
them, and seek the welfare of and ours above them and theirs (Pause)

Lord, have mercy. **Lord, forgive**

For those times when we have sought the elevation of our rights over
the rights of others, and to ignore our responsibilities to others and to
you (Pause)

Lord, have mercy. **Lord, forgive**

For those times when we have misused your gracious gifts, failing to be good stewards of all the good things that have been entrusted to us by previous generations and to leave a healthy legacy for generations to come (Pause)

Lord, have mercy. **Lord, forgive**

For those times when we have been selective in learning from your word, reluctant in following Christ, fearful in bearing the cross and slow to share your love with others (Pause)

Lord, have mercy. **Lord, forgive**

For those times when we have divided your church, brought shame on your name, and hampered the proclamation of your good news (Pause)
Lord, have mercy. **Lord, forgive**

In scripture we are told that if we confess our sins and failings, God is faithful and just, and will forgive us and make us clean, therefore where we truly repent, we can know that we are forgiven.

So in repentance we turn away from our failings in the past

<u>Act of Commitment to Reconciliation</u>

At the end of this year's 4 Corners Festival, now through the power of Christ's Spirit we commit ourselves to do what God desires,

to love as sacrificially as Christ has loved us;

to forgive as we have been forgiven;

to engage in the ministry of reconciliation;

to seek and make peace;

to speak the truth, in love;

to hope unswervingly and proclaim that hope consistently

to serve rather than be served,

to give to Caesar what is Caesar's, but to God what is God's,

to act justly and practise mercy,

and walk humbly with our God

through Jesus Christ our Lord. Amen.

[There follows a time of silence in which everyone present is invited to consider what practical action they will commit to take on in the course of the year ahead.]

Loving God, as we leave this church tonight, give us your grace. Help us to remain faithful to this commitment of peacemaking, so as to transform this wounded and wonderful city of Belfast in the here and now for the peace and prosperity of all. We ask this guided by your Spirit, through Christ our Lord, Amen.

Afterwards, Reverend Steve Stockman, Father Martin Magill and Reverend David Campton opened the proceedings to the floor, asking people for their thoughts on the festival. As Steve walked down the outer aisle and handed me the microphone, I heard a man behind me say, "In all the years I've been going to church I've never seen a minister do that. They've always been fond of keeping the microphone to themselves."

Some people beside me were talking to each other about an event in west Belfast earlier that week. "No, that was not my thing at all," said one woman. I turned to them and said how good the event had been but was dismissed with some eye-rolling for daring to join their conversation. At the refreshments afterwards, while I was speaking to a man, a woman who knew him came up to him and turned her back on me so that our conversation couldn't continue.

I looked around the room and spotted a woman I'd spoken to at the Trauma and Spirituality Conference in 2011. She was speaking, it seemed, to the same man she'd been talking to back then. I thought of all the hundreds of different churches I'd experienced since then and the effect they had had on me. I thought of the words I'd heard Jim Deeds speak earlier in the night – "With ecumenism you end up going around in circles," and wondered. It seemed to me that the thoughts of one woman I met on a course at the Irish School of Ecumenics summed up ecumenical circles. In her church she was one of the few in the congregation who attended ecumenical events. When people in her congregation were asked to go they would say, "Oh no, that's not for me," content perhaps to believe that somehow their version of God was the only one; happy to keep divisions up, to divide the Holy Spirit, content to believe that their way was the right way, perhaps. So although there are many people involved in ecumenical matters, after a while you get to see the same people over and over again.

Chapter 9: What Do I See and Feel?

"The soul understands what the eyes do not see" Rumi

Deep into my connection with printmaking I sometimes found that when I looked up at the other artists in the workshop, I could see lights around people and glowing coming from their eyes. Surprised at first, I grew used to it when I realised it seemed to happen when people were at their most connected and creative. Then I noticed the same look around congregations as they worshipped.

This was at a time when I still couldn't hear "God" without being annoyed, so I was uneasy about it, but then, shit, I thought, maybe there is something in all this God stuff after all.

I'd always been self-reliant. My inner voice always telling me to just try and figure out whatever's going on. This reliance, I think, is something to do with being the youngest of four girls and the training I received at art college on trying to discover my own personal vision. This is the same questioning mind I took back to the library where I found a pocketbook of religion. Then I came across the book *Mysticism: A Study in the Nature and Development of Spiritual Consciousness* by Evelyn Underhill. In particular the Mystic and the six stages of mysticism, the third being illumination, sometimes reached by artists – that wonderful feeling when everything you're creating gives you a direct connection with your inner being and divine self. This makes sense, I thought. All those hours of making, questioning, doing, thinking, no thought of the time, no consideration of the many hours needed to create.

In it she states: "In illumination we come to that state of consciousness which is popularly supposed to be peculiar to the mystic: a form of mental life, a kind of perception, radically different from that of 'normal' men." Later she writes: "Those who still go with him a little way—certain prophets, poets, artists, dreamers do so in virtue of that mystical genius, that instinct for transcendental reality, of which all seers and creators have some trace." Then she says:

"We have seen that all real artists, as well as all pure mystics, are sharers to some degree in the illuminated life. They have drunk, with Blake, from that cup of intellectual vision which is the chalice of the spirit of life; know something of its divine inebriation whenever Beauty inspires them to create If the mystic way be considered as an organic process of transcendence, this illuminated apprehension of things, this cleansing of the doors of perception, is surely what we might expect to occur as man moves towards higher centres of consciousness."

It's the reason why so many artists and creative people suffer all sorts of poverty and discomfort. It's as if they know that nothing else is of importance other than that deeply connected feeling and they will stop at nothing to pursue it. If you manage to get there once, it's an island you don't forget; something that nothing or no one else can feel, lost in our internal selves. It doesn't make us particularly easy to live with but it does push the world forward on a different trajectory. As the artist is never usually satisfied with the status quo.

It seemed ever clearer to me that some sort of alchemy was happening inside me. Over time the seeds you nurture with your eyes influence how you view the world and how the world sees you. It was becoming evident that not watching any media and instead spending my time in my studio or looking at art was affecting my perception. It was as if my eyes were purifying at the same time, and it felt that my body was radiating some kind of energy beyond normal human heat. Often when I was standing beside someone it felt like they were hovering in my energy. Great flows of energy would periodically swoop as if from nowhere. Once, while sitting in Saint George's Church for a service (which is amazing to take Communion in – walking past the choir like a chorus of angels), I felt as if I was being inflated like a balloon from the head downwards. What was this? Who could I ask or believe? Would I be happy with the answer?

Alistair MacLennan, recently retired senior lecturer from Belfast School of Art, is a performance artist feted around the world. Art for him has always been a spiritual practice, but in recent conversations with me he spoke of that aspect having almost been forgotten about in art-school teaching. Certainly in my own training it was never mentioned. Is the mystical insight of the artist no longer required? But then what else brings the joy that creativity can?

I rediscovered this aspect of art making at the time when massive cuts were put upon the artistic infrastructure in Northern Ireland, which have continued year-on-year in a downward spiral. Nelson McCausland, DUP MLA, was the Minister for Culture, Arts and Leisure at the time he made a visit to the Belfast Print Workshop, where until the week before I had been chairperson. Nelson is known as a person with a strong faith and I wonder if he had ever considered his proposed cuts were taking people from their spiritual practice? Why else would artists put up with so much if not to connect with the divine within?

I had come across Ralph McCutcheon, an interesting man who had trained as an engineer then kinesiologist. He was recommended to me by a friend when I had an incident at a community centre – one of the staff had verbally attacked me and left me feeling she had poured hate into me. It was a feeling I couldn't shift, which was affecting my sleeping patterns and daily existence. On my first visit he listened and then did some kinesiology adjustments. Kinesiology is a non-invasive holistic energy therapy combining the ancient principles of Traditional Chinese Medicine with modern muscle-monitoring techniques. I continued going to Ralph for some adjustments, resulting in all my symptoms disappearing. Ralph then became one of the people I went to when something felt out of balance or something was happening that I couldn't explain. Ralph said I was radiating love; the churchgoing had cleansed my inner life so much that it had found my divine core and was shining it over and over again, which resulted in this feeling of energy radiating from me. It felt like a good place to me, a very human place, by which I mean all humans are capable of developing it but sometimes it's hard to deal with. As I write this now, I feel a starburst of energy flowing down my head. Sometimes it feels like a diamond, other times a flow; sometimes soft, other times hard. While applying myself to sit down and write this book and review drafts, I can only do it in six-hour bursts as I feel so dispersed and "high" on a spiritual basis that I can't focus to type.

At a confirmation service in the Church of the Nativity with Father Pat Sheenan, it felt like fresh spiritual clarity with all the young boys and girls wearing their sashes for confirmation; when immersed with the chanting Buddhists of Nichiren Buddhism, it's like a sort of ball hardened, which is supposed to connect you into the flow of life; with the elderly congregation of Saint Patrick's Church of Ireland on the Newtownards Road, under watch of the amazing Reverend John Cunningham supported by his wife Linda, the combination of spiritual depth in the congregation makes me feel giddy and extremely light after a service, as if the combined soul energy of the people gathered amplifies my experience and lifts my spirits. The quality of the soul energy seems significant.

I didn't feel confident talking to clergy about what I was experiencing – I think because I didn't want to label myself or put it in a box. My first experiences of talking to people involved with ecumenical church matters weren't particularly good – they did listen but told me I wasn't the Dalai Lama and never replied to a follow-up that was requested. On one occasion I explained to a person working in spiritual direction what I was experiencing. When I said I sometimes wondered how people could believe some of the things they are told in church, she didn't wait to hear what things. She told me I might be doing something dangerous as churchgoing offers people psychospiritual protection and me mixing things up might be harmful. As she said it, I felt an energetic punch coming out from her solar plexus into my personal sphere. Perhaps if she'd waited for me to say that I had heard a preacher say, "… and that was why the Pope congratulated the man for killing his brother because his brother was a Protestant," she might have thought differently. I only heard it once in a Free Presbyterian church by a visiting American minister and it alarmed me. I wanted to put my hand up and ask what century he was talking about but decided not to when he pointed to me explaining how he had been saved when he had been sitting right where I was. I was wondering what exactly that felt like but people were too busy shouting, "Yes, Jesus, yes, Jesus," for me to focus.

I wondered if I was taking on too much – maybe it was affecting me? Maybe it held dangers I wasn't aware of? Ralph put my mind at rest. He told me what I was doing was so rare particularly in Northern Ireland, and not to stop.

I can understand why the woman was so protective of her belief system, but I wish she had stopped to listen – such an unusual thing in Northern Ireland. I'm often asked questions and wonder why people bother when they push in with their own answers not waiting for my reply. A friend of mine says it's because people get excited, but I think people in their trauma have forgotten how to listen. I've been told that maybe that's the essence of my work, simply objective listening. After all, you know what you're going to say, so why not listen to someone else's perspective.

One Sunday I unwittingly attended an Irish language service in Saint Mary's off Chapel Lane in Belfast, the city's oldest Catholic church built in part with financial help from Presbyterians. I took my seat and immediately the service started I felt bubbles of energy coming up from beneath me, feeling very much like the bubbles rising from a fish. I was transfixed wondering what it was. My husband had joined me on that occasion and asked if I wanted to go as we couldn't understand the service, but as the bubbles increased all I could think of was the effect the service was having on me and even though I couldn't understand it in the written word, my soul was touched. At least now I recognised I had a soul, and I went home with my energy bodies tinkling and sparkling. It was quite remarkably beautiful.

Saint Mary's attracts a devoted older congregation with lots more men than in some Catholic congregations, and with its combined energy it seemed to be connecting to something deeply ancient – something I was connecting with by being there. It's not the same in the lunchtime English speaking services or in churches abroad when attending foreign-language services, so I think it's to do with the combined energy of the people there along with the language.

The energy I felt on my first church visit has changed and it's important to note that the energy I feel each time is different depending on the congregation. While a service is going on every church seems to have its own energy, and in some I have to wait for a service to start but in others it starts immediately. For example, when I went through the church door with the Jehovah's Witnesses in north Belfast, which has a large Polish congregation, I felt a pilot light inside my head. The only other time I felt it was after a sweat lodge experience in Wicklow. Eager as I am to experience all things spiritual, I've tried it a couple of times. It originates from the Native

American tradition and would have been used a couple of times a year to spiritually cleanse and set intentions for the new season. Each time I experienced it, afterwards I felt a pilot light ignite in my head. It was as if the dross of my spirit was cleansed away and I was firmly back in sync again. Other times it's like a flow or simply love radiating from me. One of the strange things I experienced (as if this wasn't all strange enough!) was that when walking into a religious bookshop I felt the flow there as well. It was as if the actual books were generating the atmosphere. It saddens me when any of these shops close, and I could never work out if the energy came from the books or the people working in the shops, but it certainly never happens in traditional bookstores.

Chapter 10: Internet-Search Church

Up early one Sunday morning and not wanting to be prescriptive I did a Google search for early-morning Belfast church services. I came across one I'd never heard of before, and decided to go to Saint Ignatius of Antioch Orthodox on the Antrim Road. Taking over a disused Church of Ireland building, the low light and icons dominate the interior. Three people – two women and one man, were singing at the front while a couple of other people graced the interior. Glancing around the church I saw, sitting on the far side of the church, a man dressed in ornate priestly robes with sunglasses on. It looked like a snapshot from a strange Francis Bacon painting. What have I walked into this time? I thought as I sat in the pew and waited.

Someone came to explain that the sacred atmosphere in the church is enhanced by the singers singing for a couple of hours before services, but that the main service wouldn't start until later. The singing was mesmerising, so I waited for the atmosphere to build-up and the arrival of more people before the patriarch of the church started the service.

There was a very moving sermon about him ignoring the cries he had heard screaming in the night only to find out the next day that a young woman had been raped nearby. He questioned if maybe he should have gone to investigate. A lovely part of the service was an opportunity for congregants to speak out and pray in their own language. It reflected the eclectic nature of the congregation that seven people did, all in different languages – Irish and Bulgarian among other tongues.

During the service, suddenly I felt an energetic surge pushing down the inside of my body and I decided to leave the service. Feeling lightheaded I sat in the car for ten minutes before I could drive, the atmosphere of the church lingering all around me. The manifestations of my body that occurred as a result of this church visit made me question my health. It was a peculiar feeling but not so bad as to make me go to the doctors.

All this changed a few weeks later when I was walking up Cave Hill for an art performance and collapsed with darting pains in my stomach. At one point I thought I wasn't going to make it off the hillside but I managed to get myself down and my husband drove me to A & E. After the requisite wait, a doctor told me it wasn't an emergency but something was up and I should visit my GP for a referral to a consultant.

The GP told me it still wasn't an emergency and to contact them if it happened again, which it did a couple of weeks later in the middle of the night when I was caring for my father who had dementia. This time a red-flag referral got me an appointment with a specialist, where after an examination I was called back to the hospital totally unaware that I was to be told that I had womb cancer.

Hearing the word "cancer" in my own diagnosis was a startling experience, as the many people who have gone through it will tell you. After further tests it was confirmed as stage 1 C, which meant that an operation should get rid of it. They told me it was very unusual for anyone to receive the warning I did and I was lucky.

As I waited on the red-flag list for treatment, I pondered my experience of the warning I'd received in the church. I went back to the Antrim Road and told the patriarch what had happened. He told me that he had been a Methodist youth worker before moving to the Orthodox church. He said that in their church until a person is christened into it, there is a barrier. Maybe, I thought, it set off this series of events and investigations for which I was very grateful.

After the initial shock I felt in good mental health. One of my discoveries from my church trips was the ecumenical Divine Healing Ministry in Saint Anne's Cathedral, which I was consistently drawn back to. It offered immediate practical help in the form of the laying on of hands for healing. Once when I was there Reverend Dr Pat Mollan, one of the first female Church of Ireland ministers, was launching a book she had co-authored with Maureen Bennett and Helen Long: *In the Pink*, offering support for those suffering with cancer while waiting for treatment and through the different stages of hopeful recovery.

Everything else went by the wayside as I concentrated on being in the best mental health I could possibly be in while receiving my treatment. I kept up attendance at the healing services when I could, not expecting healing but galvanising my spirit for any treatment. It

56

felt like I was keeping God on my side while everything else dropped away. One of the few Christian artists I know asked if I wanted her to pray for me after I told her of my diagnosis. She held my hand and prayed a simple prayer, and as she did, I felt my spirits rise and come to a fused beingness. It was as if her spirit and mine were rising together as a physical manifestation of her prayer.

For anyone who has had a cancer diagnosis, like many of us the shock and disruption it can cause can be overwhelming. I remember my diagnosis was around the time of the Back in Belfast campaign, brought about because of the flag protests which were keeping people away from the City centre. I decided to keep participating in a work contract for bringing artists onto Belfast streets and giving their artwork away. My ego, still intact at this stage, wondered if after all the creative talent I'd been given, perhaps I would leave this Earth without having reached my full potential, but, then again, knowing that death is a good career move for artists I thought that perhaps, finally, people might take an interest in my creative output.

Luckily I was in hospital awaiting surgery quickly. I noticed there were Bibles next to each bed but no one seemed to be reading them. One lady in a bed beside me brought her own Bible and told me that her husband had been a Jehovah's Witness. After six children she had had to get away from him.

The young twenty-one-year-old woman across from me was in hospital with a complicated pregnancy. She had two children already and said she needed to have more because of a love of even numbers. Her surly, tall tracksuited boyfriend's presence felt a bit threatening, and he was often with her not sure what to do with himself. I overheard him talking about "those UVF boys coming up from Bangor".

When I was getting registered for entrance into hospital the nurse asked me if I wanted any clergy to visit. "Yes," I said. "What kind?" she asked. I said it didn't matter, that she should just put in a general request and see who turns up. She laughed and said that very few people request visits from clergy now compared to years ago, and they are usually very specific about who they want to visit.

On my last day of hospital a smiling minister came to see me. He said he'd been delighted to see that I hadn't cared which denomination the clergy visit was from as sometimes he walks towards a person and they put their hand up to refuse him. He loved what I was doing with my church visits, and as we laughed together, he asked if I wanted prayer, so there we sat in the middle of the ward with him taking my hand and saying a prayer. I felt the physical presence of the flow of prayer and became overwhelmed with tears. Here is this amazing help that is available to everyone and yet so few take up the opportunity.

I thought about the surly boyfriend who, after his girlfriend had been sent home, had found her screaming in the bath surrounded by blood. After an emergency readmittance to hospital she lost her baby and while she was on the operating table, he was told she was unable to have any more children. The young man was loitering around the corridor of the ward, still unsure what to do with himself. After he told me what had happened, I hugged him and told him how lucky he was to have two children already. He said his girlfriend's two children weren't his with tears in his eyes hanging around the bags that were already there. I thought about this young couple's suffering and the unlikelihood of them reaching out to the church community for help, or perhaps the church community reaching out to them to assist with their healing, or their inability to understand that the weight of their personal suffering could be alleviated by the church family.

I was distressed to find out that the Saint Ignatius of Antioch Orthodox Church moved from their Antrim Road location due to repairs that were needed on the building. They were sharing other spaces for worship and ritual. It concerned me to think that the build-up of sacred energy would be different – perhaps not having the same effect. But it was pleasing that they had found a more permanent home for their services in Belfast Central Mission on the third floor. If my Google search had come up any differently that day, would the sequence of events that led to my diagnosis have happened? Would I now be incubating a more progressive and difficult cancer story like many others? Thankfully my recovery was unusual: no chemotherapy was required and five years later no symptoms have returned.

Since this experience I've had family members with their own cancer journeys. During this time I've felt a physical presence of God around me and inside me. Even when I'm not asking for help it's there. Such is the amazing mystery.

58

Chapter 11: Technology and the Spirit

As I've evolved in such a way that I feel a physical impact of my spiritual practice, I'm worried about the distracting nature of technology, the screen time that Westerners deal with on a daily basis and the impact on their internal selves. In JFK Airport, New York, for the first time I saw a cafe bar with an iPad sitting vertically up in front of every customer. Looking at this and knowing I've often sat eating and drinking with my phone or iPad as my companion, it still disturbed me seeing lines of screens installed like that in a public space.

On that same trip to New York, while walking through Times Square and running the gauntlet of the mega flashing screens that gave me a headache for hours, it also got me thinking – where exactly does the life of the spirit have to develop in Times Square? I felt as if the top of my head had been chopped off – a slice going through my middle forehead, and my energy flow had disappeared, and I wondered for a while if I was destined for a life most ordinary.

The sensitivity of my spirit means that I often have to remove myself from toxic environments, ones overpowered with a hard kind of cutting energy that interferes with my inner sense of peace. But if you're unfamiliar with this possibility or don't realise that there's any other way to live, how would you know?

The alternative universe that many of the entertainment sectors offer is a constant distraction from the reality around you. Now it's moving a step further with virtual reality (VR). My first interaction with VR was at Sonic Arts Research Centre, Queens University Belfast. I watched a line of children waiting to play, and as I immersed myself in the VR experience I wondered if this fabricated outer world will simply disconnect the inner human world further from its spiritual core? Maybe we're on the cusp of losing the connection altogether? With other trials using 3D painting programmes the light is so bright when you're immersed in the experience that once the headset is removed, day-to-day reality looks even darker. The shamanic traditions teach the ancient inner essence work of vision quests – no drugs required, only drums. Close your eyes and be taken on a journey with no VR helmet required, just your inner connectedness.

On a Sunday morning at Belfast Film Festival 2018, I booked in to see the VR lab where visitors could try out different short films. There was a woman there with a six or seven-year-old child. I wondered what this experience was doing to the child's inner development? Something quite different to the children at the nearby Redeemer Central, a building gifted by the dwindling Presbyterian congregation to an emerging vibrant family cafe-style church that overflows with communal energy and vitality.

The flashing lights of the TV and the love affair with mobile phones offer up an altogether different possibility. Are oversized TVs and constant distraction simply a way to try and keep humans trapped inside a consumerist hell? Loneliness is rife in our Western world and advertisers are well known for playing on desires, and the media obsession with youth forms a distorted focus on what is desirable. Material possessions and the pursuit of the have-it-all Western mentality are king. It's easy to set yourself adrift in the ocean of consumerism and distraction and forget about the life of the spirit – I did for many years, yet how many times have you heard people say, "I can't help thinking there is something else?" If something is whispering to your soul, how could you tell without having enough silence and space to hear it? "Be still and know that I am God" is often up on the walls of older church buildings – ancient wisdom and good advice.

To be clear I am not a luddite, in 2018 I completed a digital futures course at Digital Arts Studios Belfast which was designed to update artists in all manner of augmented reality/ virtual reality etcetera. I am deeply aware of the seduction and excitement around such using such tools. Yet there might be good reason to pause. Luckily there is a trend to see beyond this consumerist idea we've been sold. A strong awareness of ecological living and environmental awareness is being nurtured around the world, but will we turn off our screens – and will that help revive the life of the spirit?

Chapter 12: Papa Francesco

My husband was looking for somewhere to go for his fiftieth birthday and I reminded him that he'd always liked Italy. "Rome," he said, "I'd like to spend some time in Rome but only if you don't spend all your time in churches."

I first visited Rome as a twenty-year-old interrailer with a backpack. Visits to the Sistine Chapel and the Colosseum are all that I remember in the hot, hot August heat. Queues formed an important part of that visit, what, if anything, had changed?

My husband researched ways of getting into a service with the Pope, because, after all, it was Rome. He came across a fax number that we could request a ticket, and for a couple of days before leaving for Italy he tried to send a fax only to consistently get an engaged message.

We arrived at our rented apartment close to the Vatican and made our way past the holy-postcard-and-calendar sellers for a first look at Saint Peter's Square. We found a queue where we could wait to convert a fax into a ticket for the Pope's general audience. Everyone else queuing had a fax but as we never received a reply, we had nothing. "Ask the angels for some help with this. I'm sure there are some hanging around here," my husband said. Eventually we arrived at the front of the queue and he explained in Italian that we had no fax and that the Pope's audience was on his birthday – showing his passport as proof. The official motioned to the Swiss guard standing beside him who pulled two tickets from his stripy tunic. Off we went only to realise we had no idea what the tickets were for or where to go for the Mass the next day. We went back and asked the guard, who told us to arrive before seven the next morning if we wanted to get a good seat, that this Pope liked to be outside and that our tickets were for St Peter's Square.

Not quite making it so early the next day, we found hundreds of people already queuing at Saint Peter's Square. A perfunctory security check into the square gave us access to seats laid out for the service. The sun was blaring, pilgrims from all around the world sat with their banners waiting in anticipation for *Papa Francesco* – Pope

Francis. We sat down and I spent some time with my watercolours and sketchbook.

The scene was set for Pope Francis with a priest calling out the names and countries that tour groups were coming from, and each group cheered as they heard their name mentioned. Suddenly a hubbub was heard in the crowd on the right-hand side. The Pope had arrived in motorised transport, stopping to kiss babies and bless people every now and then; his security detail running behind him. A circuit lined with barriers that ran through the crowd made it easier for him to roam where he wanted, much to the delight of the crowd. When he came close to us, I felt a surge in the energy of the crowd as everyone moved towards him shouting, "*Papa! Papa!*" He smiled broadly and seemed to enjoy the entire spectacle in a very carefree way.

The Pope made his way up to a stage in front of Saint Peter's and the service started with priests translating into seven languages. Each time congregants couldn't understand a particular language, they waited in respectful silence until their turn came. At the end of the service it was explained that the Pope had decided to do a special blessing at his Masses that would reach not only the people who were present, but also their families at home and any religious artefacts we had with us. The blessing was written in Latin on the back of the entrance tickets. As everyone repeated it, the crowd filled up with raised spirits. They say at Easter or when a new Pope is being inaugurated four hundred thousand can fill the square. This day probably only one hundred thousand people were there for Mass – the largest congregation I've ever been part of. The combined energy of that congregation stayed with me for days afterwards.

After the service we went to the Vatican post office and bought postcards and stamps. Adding addresses to my family on the back I hastily wrote: *You have just been blessed by the Pope whether you like it or not*. One of my sisters, who lives in a predominantly Protestant area, later told me I'd got the wrong address on her card. A neighbour came to her door with the postcard saying that it had been dropped in her letterbox by mistake. My sister turned the postcard to see the Pope looking back at her. It made me chuckle!

There was also the opportunity to go to the Papal Blessing while we were there. Unsure if I would go, I woke on the Sunday with a feeling of linear energy flowing intensely down into my forehead and a strong emotion that it would be a good idea to attend the blessing. It was a much quicker event, with the Pope at his apartment balcony. He ended with a request for us all to go off and enjoy our Sunday dinner. It felt familiar and weirdly parochial somehow.

The rest of our time in Rome I kept noticing the locations of the early churches; more specifically the post-Reformation churches that were built to make the Catholic Church look ever more impressive. I thought about the power that religion has had throughout the ages and the impact the Reformation would have had on such a city. Walking around the jail of an ancient Pope's I couldn't help but imagine the reasons why people were imprisoned in the past.

I thought about the congregation from all over the world in Saint Peter's Square. I've sometimes heard people say the Catholic Church's influence is coming to an end and that no one goes to Mass any more, but I saw in Rome that Catholicism has no intention of going away and we in Northern Ireland are just a strange leftover from previous centuries' fallouts and fights that just keep rumbling on like the long tail of another bloody battle.

I thought about the population of Rome: nearly three million people with nine hundred churches compared to the Belfast population of nearly three hundred thousand and four hundred-odd churches – how had this come about?

Chapter 13: Communion

"You mean there are Protestants sitting around a Belfast bap on a weekday lunchtime having Communion?" were a friend's shocked words when I started to talk about Communion I'd experienced.

"That one was at a weekend," I replied.

One aspect of church-hopping is an interest in the different ways church denominations have evolved to do the same thing. With a decentralisation of decisions, rituals have evolved in different ways. Take Communion, for example. According *to Wikipedia: "Communion (sacrament) or Eucharist or the Lord's Supper is the Christian rite involving the eating of bread and drinking of wine, reenacting the Last Supper."* Whether you're asked to the front of the church or a plate is passed around, the communal experience links back to the Last Supper.

At first I wouldn't take it, but one day in Saint Anne's Cathedral I walked up, almost against my own will, and kneeled at the rail. So how is this performed in different churches? The Roman Catholic Church offers it every week, as do some of the reformed churches on weekdays, while other reformed churches perform it once a month.

Let's look at the drinking of wine. As the early Church grew, wine for Communion was limited to the priest, due to the difficulty in obtaining it, but during the Reformation the Protestant Church insisted on it being introduced. Even with that, I've received a great number of variations – on two occasions I've been offered wine in a Roman Catholic Church service, and I understand this isn't the rule. It was given from a chalice after the priest, and interestingly was white wine, not red. The type and variation of the wine or liquid given in the reformed churches is as varied as the churches themselves. The best-quality wine for Communion is served in Down Cathedral from a chalice. The Church of Ireland always offers communion wine from a chalice, for which you form an orderly queue to receive, kneeling along the altar rails at the front of the church. Some Baptist, Methodist and Presbyterian or "Christian-labelled" churches prefer the small individual glasses of wine handed around on a tray while the congregation remains seated in the pews or their seats (but I've also received it up at the altar). I've had blackcurrant juice and a number of other difficult-to-identify red juices as a substitute for wine. In one gospel hall I was offered a small glass of tap water for Communion. In a Methodist church I thought I'd come across something new when the visiting minister said that if anyone didn't want Communion, they could leave while it was happening. At that particular church it was traditional for communicants to be prayed over at the altar. As the congregation was large this took a long time, and as I found out on leaving, "Some people like to get home and get their dinner instead."

Sometimes in small congregations the pastor, minister or priest states that everyone is welcome to have Communion if they accept Jesus. On occasions they indicated to me while saying it, so as a visitor I knew where I stood. Instructions on Communion are given from the front; in some Baptist churches they tell visitors that it's the tradition of the church to wait until everyone has been given wine before the whole congregation takes Communion together. In one gospel hall I attended, my juice went down the wrong way and brought me into a coughing fit to which the elderly woman sitting in front of me said she wondered why that had happened and looked at me knowingly. This is the same church that I took my friend Suellen to, and she said the congregation was so still that if the women just took their hats off and shaved their heads it reminded her of a group of Zen nuns because they were so quiet. Interestingly, it had never crossed my mind, not having had the experience myself.

When I took someone who was Catholic to a Church of Ireland Communion service, they would get up once given bread, thinking it was the end, only to be nudged back into place to wait for the wine. Many of the churches that use small glasses or plastic thimble-sized cups to serve the wine or juice have holes or containers in the church furniture to hold the receptacle after Communion is taken. In some churches I've experienced a tray or a number of trays of wine coming around the room and congregants just lift a cup themselves in a less formal manner, sometimes accompanied by music, sometimes not.

The variety of bread or host is almost as variable as the wine. In Roman Catholic churches a host, or small round disc of unleavened bread is used. It's kept on a silver tray and given by either the priest or the extraordinary minister of Holy Communion. The communicants queue up, pew by pew, ready to proceed to the front or halfway towards the front, and an orderly flow back into the pew is usually successful. Sometimes congregants leave directly afterwards. At one outdoor Mass in Falls Park, west Belfast, during the Féile an Phobail festival, the priest ran out of host due to the large amount of people who turned up for the outdoor experience. He said, "This is what it must have felt like when Jesus was feeding the multitude." Thankfully he had a reserve in his bag for the occasion.

It felt like such a privilege to sit among the community of west Belfast who were just out enjoying their Sunday. I wondered how people who still have a perception of west Belfast being a dangerous place would have felt about the experience.

Priests sometimes comment at funerals that if the congregation don't feel they can take Communion but would like a blessing they can come up with their hands folded across their chest. One priest in Andersonstown told the congregation he had been presiding over a funeral and when it was time for receiving Communion, congregants were almost snatching the host out of his hands, so much was the feeling of entitlement from those gathered. He reminded people that they should be prayerful in receiving it.

Other offerings during Communion have been grapes or boxes of raisins for children, and in one United Methodist service in Chicago on World Aids Day people were invited to take a red commemoration ribbon for Aids as well as communion bread from the same tray. Twice it was brown bread, not wheaten, but a pale light brown sliced loaf or granary. Once it was a piece of crumbled Scottish shortbread – I didn't ask if it was leftovers from Christmas two weeks previous and if they used it all year around! Gluten-free has also been offered – although I've noticed recently that the Catholic Church have stopped this practice.

At the Adoration Chapel on the Falls Road with its Perpetual Eucharistic Adoration run by the Adoration Sisters there is a large circular host encased in glass in a monstrance on the altar. The nuns make their living from baking the altar bread and there is one that stays in the chapel in perpetual adoration.

The chapel is open from 6 a.m. until midnight every day and other hours by appointment. Anyone can join the sisters at prayer times or during the week there is a Mass at noon every day. The first time I visited it was Easter and there was standing room only. Unusually, no service sheet was given but there was singing by the whole congregation. The small chapel filled with a calm, spiritual presence. I mentioned this at a church in east Belfast after I noticed how they put out a bowl of crusty bread and some wine to dip it in for Communion. After the service, as I was shown around their building, someone was feeding the leftover bread to the kids and then chucking any remains into the bin. It made for an interesting discussion and some contemplation on how the Communion ritual differs in each church.

In three church services I've been refused Communion. In one gospel hall on the Shankill Road, with only three people at the service, I was asked when I entered if I was born-again. When the question was repeated I said that there were many ways towards Jesus, which meant that the Communion ritual swiftly skipped me. In another service I was welcomed in but told at the beginning that I wouldn't be offered Communion because I had to agree to their principles. If I did so, I could be welcomed into the Communion ritual in the future. I accepted whatever guidance I was given by anyone; aware that different denominations see preparation for the ritual as important in different ways.

"God's bouncers" was the name I gave to two men who refused me entry into one church. They told me I needed a letter and I told them I just wanted to go to church. Eventually they said I could attend the service but would have to sit with the young girl at the back and not take Communion. There were about ten people in a beautifully stripped-back room in a square sitting with a Belfast bap in the middle. During the service, which was taken by different men in attendance, I was welcomed and apologised to. The communion bap quickly moved past me, and at the end of the service I was apologised to again and invited for Sunday dinner by the man who had initially refused me entry. I thanked him but didn't go. On leaving I felt such a great sense of expanded consciousness that I could hardly drive. I believe it was the result of being with a small group with lifetimes devoted to God.

Something else to note about the bread offered during Communion is that thankfully it has never been stale. Belfast baps are popular but pan loaf cut into squares is a favourite. Sometimes communicants are welcome to tear a piece off and other times not.

Once I started taking Communion again, only twice have I felt unable to take it; the first time being in the Orthodox church. A large icon was being held at the front by the patriarch and before taking Communion people kissed it. I just didn't feel I could do it. The second time was in my home village of Strangford in a chapel. For some reason I didn't feel I could do it in front of the people I had grown up with who knew I hadn't been brought up a Catholic.

And so the ritual continues. Some people are shocked when I tell them I take Communion from any denomination and wonder what they think might happen to me, yet I never feel the worse for it and have managed to survive up until now – never bursting into flames, as someone suggested to me, or getting sick because of it.

Chapter 14: Administering God

One fascinating aspect of a church's existence is the way different denominations have been administered and the effect on congregations being able to survive today. During the thirteen years I set up and ran cross-community cross-border development programmes, it was my gift to come across many people whom I wouldn't have had the opportunity to connect with before. Quite honestly – in earlier periods of my life it would have been dangerous to do so.

One such person was Brian Quinn. I came across Brian when working in north Belfast helping Intercomm, the cross-community development agency on the Antrim Road. I had helped set up a programme for women to develop business ideas – firstly with Nora Quigley, then Maria McEntee. Brian Quinn and I were used to having very honest conversations about politics, and I enjoyed the verbal sparring. I saw the difficulty of getting people to switch off their warrior instincts after years of being enemies, particularly where there were still real threats made by dissident groups.

I remember telling Brian about a local women where I grew up, when the local GAA had given out wooden blocks to pensioners as Christmas gifts, had thrown them back and said she didn't want their Fenian blocks. In return he told me a republican mantra was that if it took a hundred years, they would run all the Protestants out of Ireland. "Not very politically correct," I remember saying. "Where's your equality agenda there?"

Over the years we bumped into each other and Brian was interested in my church visits, letting me know about unusual services he came across to see if I knew about them. He invited me to a commemoration service held in the Dockers Club led by a Catholic priest and Presbyterian minister. The priest joked that he didn't bring his wife with him while the minister did! The Presbyterian minister talked on the importance of memory – how Presbyterians forget that they didn't have rights and Catholics forget that they fought in World War One. But it was the experience of the procession to Saint Joseph's that really struck me. Saint Joseph's was a Catholic church in the Sailortown area of Belfast that had been closed for being unsustainable. Some who felt abandoned and betrayed by the Church campaigned to reopen it. People talked of skips turning up and church statues being thrown into them, which angered the past congregation.

A group of devoted campaigners held a Mass every Sunday outside the church, before eventually moving to the upstairs of a building close by. Brian told me of the procession held in honour of Our Lady of Fátima, which started in the Marian year of 1954. Local children getting confirmed walked in front of the chapel's statue of the Virgin Mary, held high on a platform of flowers on the shoulders of men from the area. Arriving on the Sunday in question, the organising committee expertly brought out the statue and a group of women followed behind while a few young girls in confirmation dress were in front. The men, including Brian, carried the statue. As we walked around the dock area, where once there were streets of houses but now there's nothing but car parks and ramshackleness with a few houses, it was a strange feeling watching this group re-enact memories of their youth with some saying the rosary. I walked along beside them and could feel the streaming energy of their prayers as they channelled – what exactly – grace? I'd never been part of an experience like this before and returned home in a pensive state.

It only started to make real sense to me after seeing a photo of the procession on Facebook taken many years before with hundreds of people taking part, and there at the front was the same man only much younger.

Saint Joseph's has since had a fundraising drive to fix the chapel roof. The art collective Household took over the derelict site for Culture Night and installed artwork and now have a long-term commitment with the area. But you can't help noticing that with the Catholic Church making decisions more centrally, the congregation had little say in Saint Joseph's closing. Compare this to the administration of the Presbyterian Sinclair Seaman's Church around the corner, still open to this day, with a small congregation in control. It continues to offer a spiritual presence in the area. The interior is a museum of all things nautical – from ships' bows to rum-ration containers, which I mistook for collection plates. There is a dedicated group of men and women who have the freedom to maintain the church and keep it operational. On speaking to them after a service I attended, one of them told me how as a child he remembers being stoned by other youths while coming to church. The church was founded by a rich trading family and one of its founding fathers also helped design the Ulster Covenant.

Going back to how God is administered in these two instances, it has given rise to different opportunities for local congregations to simply have a functioning church or not.

In another part of the city's Folktown, Berry Street Presbyterian Church had a very small congregation when I started this odyssey and it closed in 2017 – the threat of the nearby shopping centre continuously wanting to gobble it up. Recently I became aware of a group calling themselves Central Church who have been given use of the space for worship and outreach. Attending the evening service, I took comfort that they had decided to hold their services in a small hall on the property with a large window looking onto the pedestrian precinct beside it. While the service took place, people wandered past and looked on at the glow that came from both the people inside and the room. There were more people outside Maddens Bar around the corner than inside the church, but it was a presence none the less.

Congregants told me that at their Christmas carol service a packed room encouraged streams of passers-by to join them, and they beckoned them in with open doors. When I visited, the church was awaiting a decision to see if they could continue using the building. Perhaps they might be gifted it?

The nearby Catholic Saint Mary's Church is one of the most used churches in the city centre. With a least one Mass every day, its bells ring out into the city and it is a place of pilgrimage and solace for many. If you think religion is on its way out, just sit in the chapel for a day and watch people coming and going, lighting candles and connecting with their spiritual selves. Spend some time in one of the pews and wonder what it's all about.

Dependence and independence, centralised administrations, breakaway churches all mean that there is a range of different ways to administer God. That they all have God at their core at least points to a similarity.

And what of gospel halls? I'd always looked at them from the outside in as a relic of a bygone age, some old-fashioned world that was out of step with contemporary reality, yet I'd never dared cross their thresholds before my churchgoing odyssey. All independent, they are, however, mostly linked as an assembly of gospel halls across the UK and world totalling twenty-six thousand assemblies worldwide. They have no salaried or ordained ministers, priests or pastors and rely on the Bible for their authority. Crescent Church is possibly the largest church congregation in this category, situated in the university area of Belfast. Their website states:

> In the New Testament, a local church consisted of Christians in a given locality, but now there is practically no complete expression of this principle. Nevertheless, in accordance with the teaching of the New Testament, Christians may meet together and function as an independent, self-governing church recognising the authority of God's word, the Lordship of Christ and the sovereignty of the Holy Spirit.

This is one gospel halls interpretation, there are variations but usually they have this central belief at their core: no bishops or archbishops, canons, fathers or very reverends – simply people and their Bibles. I always come away from them feeling incredibly present and crystal clear. I've had some interesting experiences crossing their thresholds. Certainly, the congregations are small, except Crescent Church, but they hold a very strong presence in terms of spiritual vibration. What do I mean by that? I've talked before about feeling a physical spiritual presence – in fact, it was one of the reasons I started out on my church journey.

When you come across a group, who come together to sit in the presence of God, who've been practising their own form of Christianity for a long time and they're all in the same room, their combined energy has an effect on anyone who sits among them. In gospel halls they usually dress up in their Sunday best outfits: men in suits and women in dresses or skirts, mostly with a hat. In one such hall, as I sat beside a lady in her eighties, I thought about how long she had been practising her spiritual instruction and who it was that she received it from. That long, spiritual stream of faith and practice I linked together as if she was holding the gauntlet from another age.

Ballyhackamore Gospel Hall in east Belfast is a great example. Small in numbers, the combined energy of the congregation gave me the feeling of expanding into another consciousness. When I returned to the car after calling into Tesco for a paper, I suddenly realised why there had been such a lobby in Northern Ireland to keep shops closed on Sundays. I had to sit in the car for ages before being able to drive. We are at a point in the Western world where perhaps we're in danger of losing the world of the spirit entirely. Take the Good Friday licensing laws and the lobbying to get them scrapped, stating that tourists need a glass of wine with their lunch and that the way people who fancy a drink are treated is inhuman. I've heard of people having a day trip to Scotland just to get a drink and avoid the laws. I think: it's just one day. Maybe people are so far from anything to do with the spirit that the act of not drinking on one Friday afternoon a year might be something positive to consider. I'm old enough to remember when all pubs were closed every Sunday and it was only hotels and clubs that were open for people to get a drink. In 2018 the Good Friday licensing laws changed in the south of Ireland to allow normal opening. Who would have suspected that in 2018 Northern Ireland was the last bastion of the Holy Spirit?

There is some great singing in gospel halls. In one I was gifted their small hymn book to take with me and told that they're a great source of strength when used. In many gospel halls it isn't the locals who are attending, but a congregation who travels from others parts of the city or outside of it entirely. Often it is because of family ties with the area – the daughter of the founder of a hall in south Belfast is still to be found in the congregation playing the piano. On hearing this I couldn't help but think that if she had been born male, perhaps she would have been up in front of the congregation. Patriarchal attitudes filtering into every aspect of the faith journey are significant in every era as to women's role in church.

It's true, however, to say that the congregations within gospel halls tend to be older. Within the next twenty years I expect there will be closures. The spiritual streams of knowledge might come to an end, but for the time being they are there to connect with. An elderly man in a congregation on the Shankill told me he used to go to a gospel hall but the numbers got so small that eventually it closed, and they joined the nearest Baptist church instead. "It's such a pity people don't want to go to church," he said. An elder of the church heard him and said, "I keep telling Jimmy that the Holy Spirit will never leave the Earth. In places like Africa the church is thriving, it's just here it's not."

An architect friend once told me that churches in urban planning are placed within cities to bring about community cohesion. When you look at a map of the Shankill and circle every church there are so many that you can't get any cohesion, yet I've found the church congregations on the Shankill to have great spiritual energy. Their diversity in worship sometimes boggles the mind but the fun and resilience they've developed is quite astounding. The light they hold within a broken city is a credit to the resilience of the human spirit. Shankill Community Fellowship Church is thriving in a building that used to belong to the UDA. The Church of God in a converted fire station throbs with swirling life as the pastor and congregation clap and sing.

The only place of worship I've almost been refused entry into was a gospel hall. In this same building a year or so later I noticed a sign outside saying there was an exhibition inside. I walked in and there were a number of free-standing boards around the room explaining their strand of Christianity with some home-made sculptures in the middle.

An elderly man explained that he and a friend were touring the exhibition around Northern Ireland. He started to explain the meaning of the panels, rhyming off each one with an authority that was in his mind absolute – there was no room for questions or queries. He told me they had tried to get it into local schools but weren't successful. Down round Newry they had had more luck with hundreds of people coming to see the exhibition.

About halfway round the exhibition I queried something he said, looking for more detail, but he ignored it and kept talking. When I asked again, he put his hand to his ear and admitted he was hard of hearing and didn't catch what I was saying. I thought at the time that this was very much people's experience of religion in Northern Ireland: being told something and not allowed to ask questions.

After the tour we sat down in the main gospel hall and had a cup of tea. He asked me how I'd feel if I died that minute – where would I go? I replied that if I died, I died. I'd had a good life and then it would be over. My mobile rang and I went outside to answer it. On arriving back the man said that he'd never experienced anyone reply as I did to his question. The church has recently been taken over by a new congregation and the signage changed to more contemporary.

Within gospel halls I'm sometimes asked to sit at the side or in a certain place, away from the inner core sitting in a square around a Communion table. The men seem to spontaneously stand up and recite from the Bible between silences and hymn singing selected by the gathered worshippers. The silences are particularly beautiful – the groups very much like Buddhist sanghas gathered to support each other, to listen to holy words and offer spiritual resilience to the outside world. With Buddhism being a more recent addition of a religion flourishing in Northern Ireland, gospel halls without suits and women in hats have much in common with them. The congregation inside gospel halls glow with a spiritual light developed over decades, and enjoy times at Christmas and Easter when they all get together from across the city in the Presbyterian Assembly halls.

During the five hundredth anniversary of the Reformation I attended a talk at Ulster University. An audience member asked the assembled panel where in the Bible it says humans need a mediator between them and God – I had seen the questioner in a gospel hall. The women on the panel said nowhere and this, to me, is the ethos that gospel halls share. After visiting any gospel hall, for days afterwards I feel further wedged into the life of the Spirit.

There are, of course, many independent churches in Belfast, and thinking back to different church's historical connections with land, property or other earthly matters means that there have been many fights and political manoeuvrings in the name of the Church. But taken as a whole it means that now there are many different structures and ways to administer God. Sometimes it's only the structure itself that exists with hardly any congregation, yet new ones are popping up all the time.

Chapter 15: Spiritual Psychology and the Divine Feminine

In 2014 I got to a stage where I needed to be with other people somewhere I could trust the discussion and feel supported. Something more in-depth was required to broaden the knowledge base of what I was already experiencing, but not tie me to any specific denomination because my feeling was that if I did that, immediately every other denomination would block my findings or observations. The burden of history between different denominations kept raising its head and trauma was keeping it in place.

An artist has a rare position in society with some of us, but not all of us, choosing to keep the integrity of our creative observations above all else. I felt that this needed protected.

A leaflet on my desk kept appearing at the top of my papers: Living Campus, Foundation in Spiritual Psychology. It was a year-long self-development seminar and the course blurb talked of integrating psychology and spirituality, Rudolf Steiner's science of the spirit, anthroposophy and the work of transpersonal psychologists, Carl Jung, Roberto Assagioli and others. Themes on the promotional leaflet included:

Psychology and spirituality

Integrating spiritual practice and psychological insight

Mapping human consciousness

Dreams, images and symbols (the language of the unconscious)

Meditation in modern life

The inner theatre (the many roles we play)

The inner child in adult life

Relationship, empathy and karma

The shadow

Polarity and the soul (seeking dynamic balance)

The inner masculine and feminine

Illness and healing

The development of the compassionate observer

Heart thinking and higher ego

Suellen thought it might be useful for me but said it was unusual to have all that content together – it wouldn't be found in the States, for instance. What I discovered, however, were two amazing psychologists inviting people on an experiential journey over the period of a year, or two with an advanced certificate in the second year.

The commitment of one Saturday a month along with a residential format suited the work I was doing, and the time to think about different aspects of spiritual life facilitated by experts in this particular stream of spiritual knowledge was very important on my journey. The course offered support and space in which to start and make sense of the journey I was on and ponder the imponderable.

Martin Donnelly and Linda McKeown have an expertise and skill set unusual in its development, but it's my personal belief that it is critical at this time on Earth. Linda has worked for over twenty years as a transpersonal development facilitator and is engaged in the ongoing process of integrating her training in transpersonal psychology with Rudolf Steiner's anthroposophy. Martin, with over twenty years' experience in the same field, is also a singer-songwriter. I hope they both are able to have time to share their wisdom further.

I also completed an adult education course at Queen's called In Search of the Divine Feminine facilitated by Dr Grace Clunie, one of the first female Church of Ireland ministers to be ordained (now connected to the Centre for Celtic Spirituality, Armagh) and Kate Fitzpatrick, author, healer and environmentalist. The combination of investigation into how the early Christian and shamanic practices held the divine feminine in different eras was also vital for my spiritual understanding. It was interesting to hear that there are shamans in Ireland who have been working to lift a perceived curse on the land – one kept in place perhaps for generations, to understand Sheela na gigs, Desert Mothers, radical nuns, abbots, mystics, druids biblical and ancient Celtic characters in more dept. One of my favourite rememberings from the start of the course was from Grace saying how a person went to one of the main religious libraries famous for its archive and looked in its index under the word "Women" only to find nothing there. It would be also lovely to see these two women write a book about what we learnt on the course.

These courses and connections gave me an understanding of the different ways the world of the Spirit has been explained or mapped out in different eras. It was interesting to see how some of Rudolf Steiner's spiritual exercises are exactly things you get taught in a traditional art college education. Rudolf Steiner also thought that Christianity was just at the beginning and that Ireland in particular had an important role to play in the spiritual development of the world. Are we perhaps moving into a new state of consciousness – is that what I was experiencing? Does anyone else feel it too?

Chapter 16: Art Pieces Inspired by the Experience

If I hadn't stopped working in North City Business Centre and started to made art none of this would have happened. If, when I collapsed, I had taken medication to keep going, instead of working my way out of that job, none of this would have happened. Connecting with other artists helped me remember that simply to create is such a magical and important thing. But even then, there was and still is opposition.

I attended a Women's conference at Belfast School of Art – there was a curated exhibition and I somehow got included. I turned my nose up at a sewing workshop held by a South American workshop facilitator who was involved in smuggling scenic squares depicting atrocities in her native land out of the country, but felt compelled to do it. Mary Hughes was sitting beside me, and we were asked to make a square of something we thought was important that people didn't know about. In silence I made a square showing me and what I felt was happening to me on an energetic basis. It was all golds and yellows and brightness and light. I felt calm after completing it but exhausted and went home and slept. This is a taste of the process that art therapists use in helping people to process their experiences.

The sacrifices people make to pursue their passion of art is mind-boggling. Sometimes people ask condescendingly, "But can you make enough to live off?" "That depends," I reply, "on whether it's only money you require to help you really live."

It was easy for me to tell myself that what I was doing was research for an art project with visiting the churches– just a thread I was following. The challenge was what would be the physical art manifestation of my experiences. What would I develop and how might people react? Truth be told I was less worried about people's reactions than developing the art pieces. The creative urge can be a difficult beast to wrangle with. It can demand you go somewhere with a sensitive subject that you can't quite articulate but that's the art part of it. It's often out of reach, just beyond grasp. The art is in making it manifest, and how people react is all part of the fun or nightmare.

It was at this time that I had my space in City East Business Centre at the bottom of the Newtownards Road. I remember the day I chose to start creating: 29 October, my birthday. The voluntary work I was doing was taking up too much of my energy and I needed to do something for myself for a change and over a period of two and a half years *The Ebb and Flow of East Belfast* was it. This involved going to the nearest newsagent on the loyalist Newtownards Road and then to a newsagent on the republican Short Strand where I bought all the newspapers for that day.

I made an etching plate of a view from the City East building – or if I was in Strangford a view from there. After making the plate I scanned the papers and purely on instinct selected fragments of news, finally handprinting a small series of etchings from each day selected using Chine-collé technique, "Chinese collage". The experience made me look in depth at our newspaper media content and the way that content reflects our views or triggers our hostilities. Or perhaps both. The experience cleansed my visual perception and the physical process of printmaking cleared out the vicarious trauma, and at the end of the two and a half years I no longer felt like the same person being pushed around like flotsam and jetsam by the media of the day.

The exhibition was first shown in the Engine Room Gallery (when it was on the Newtownards Road), run by Cliff Brooks and Joanne Jamison. The reaction of the general public was quite overwhelming. Some people laughed, some cried, one person even wanted to rip it off the wall. People said it felt very east Belfast as they brought in the feeling from the street when they came to view the exhibition. Subsequently it was shown in The Saint Patrick Centre in Downpatrick, where people said it was very County Down; and in Cultúrlann in west Belfast, as part of the Féile an Phobail, viewers said it was very west Belfast. For the centenary of the Easter Rising commemorations in Dublin I was invited to show a selection of the series in the Irish Architectural Archive.

During that time, it was actually pretty quiet on the Newtownards Road, particularly on a Sunday when it returned to feeling like a village without any commuter traffic. Resigning from my position as chair of the Belfast Print Workshop, I started the online community hub Creative Change NI, which connected artists and galleries across Northern Ireland (but particularly Belfast) on a voluntary basis. I won a Digital Heroes Award for my work and was invited to Westminster Parliament to collect it.

Noticing a call-out for views on an arts festival for east Belfast, I invited all my members. The ensuing meeting about the festival was filled with creative energy, created in part by my members who lifted the energy of the meeting to a can-do mentality. Digital media was enabling communication across social media platforms in a way that had previously never been possible. Connections and communications speeded up and as nobody owns cyberspace it allowed for new possibilities to be made.

All year I thought about what I would do in the EastSide Arts Festival and how we might a shift the energy in the area. I curated an exhibition in City East along with workshops and a talk, but it was the performative walk *Lament*, developed in conjunction with Suellen, that really had a lasting impact. Using the festival brochure, we invited people to a walking meditation performance at the bottom of the Newtownards Road on a Sunday afternoon. The flashpoint location having experienced so much violence and tension over the last hundred years. We were unsure if anyone would turn up, but around twenty people did – one person so stiff with fear at the location that she stood apart from the group and said she felt it was too much for her to join us any further. It was only days afterwards that we realised that everyone who had attended had a spiritual belief of some sort.

We introduced ourselves and Elvina Porter McCullough, who was commissioned to film the walk. I spoke of my visits to local churches and Suellen talked of her experience of walking the Camino de Santiago and explained what a walking meditation was, how to do it and what we were going to do.

As we practised the walking meditation, we handed breath poems to anyone who wanted to read one out. I carried a large mixing bowl filled with hydrangeas and Suellen led the walk off the grass and onto the Newtownards Road. At places of her choosing we stopped by the ring of a mindfulness bell and someone read a breath poem. I offered participants the bowl of flowers and they chose a flower and set it somewhere ritualistically.

We crossed the road and circled Saint Mathew's, the Catholic church on the opposite side, then continued up the road stopping periodically; at one point under a bus shelter to share a bag of organic apples to eat mindfully. Video footage shows walkers sniffing their apples and connecting in the desolate urban environment.

Passing Freedom Corner and the paramilitary murals in the area it was clear that the walk was affecting people in different ways. Few others were around except the odd person stopping in a car to get out with shopping. Back down where we started, we gathered into a circle holding hands. Suellen asked for a word about the experience. Many were "joyful", "spiritual experience" but the two clergies were "dark" and "darkness" was another one. We stood around hugging each other and talking about it afterwards. I felt as if my insides had been scraped out.

Two years later we still hadn't edited the footage as we were unsure what exactly we'd done. The invitation to show it at the Sullivan Galleries in Chicago forced us to look at it again. We exhibited the edited footage with a church pew for viewers to watch from. It was strange for me to explain to people in downtown Chicago why exactly the location was so contentious, why we had shot the footage that was so evocative, so powerful, in people's minds, why so few people walked in the area and the mental baggage people had about being in the area.

By a strange coincidence, the Lord Mayor of Belfast at the time, Máirtín Ó Muilleoir, Sinn Féin, was coming to Chicago, and we invited him to see our exhibition. He immediately recognised the priest in the footage as Father Martin Magill and easily understood the significance of the location of our art piece. We had a good chat about the contribution that churches were making in Belfast and the innovation and outreach they were doing. "What have you seen?" he asked. I liked the way he asked then actually listened. It was his experience that it was the churches that were reaching out to the most vulnerable in the city. I've heard him say since that he was surprised by the support he personally received from the churches. But they are so full of love and forgiveness.

Back in Belfast six months or so later I was installing the first visual arts exhibition in the new Duncairn Centre for Culture and Arts, a converted Presbyterian church, in north Belfast run by the 174 Trust when I noticed Father Martin Magill having coffee. After introducing myself, he recognised me and asked me how much the *Lament* walk had affected me. We agreed to meet and talk about it, and at our subsequent meeting Father Martin told me how he had gone home after the walk and for days felt extremely affected by the emotions it churned up for him. He used the experience for his sermon the following week as well as commenting on it during a radio broadcast. He said he never knew a piece of art could have such a profound effect on someone; how the act of physically being in an unfamiliar part of the city with historical and political baggage could shift his perception of a place. He told me that *Lament* was one of the reasons he and Reverend Steve Stockman of Fitzroy Presbyterian started the 4 Corners Festival – an annual series of events encouraging members of religious congregations in the city to participate in something interesting in a part of the city they're unfamiliar with; hoping to and succeeding in building the community and acting as a bridge for understanding. That Suellen and I had developed an art piece that had contributed to such a festival was mind-blowing. I often talk about it when people ask what the outcome of art is – that is apart from saying, "How long have you got?"

We talked about participating in the next 4 Corners Festival, and I suggested two possibilities: firstly, over the time I'd been visiting churches I'd noticed a small number of artists in Belfast who were dealing with the subject of religion and spirituality in their artwork. These works had never been curated together before and I thought that showing this work together was a good idea to help open discussion around religion in an interesting way. This happened in 2015 and the festival used it as their opening night in north Belfast. Secondly, I wanted to do something with the churches themselves. After some discussion with Martin and Steve, I came up with the idea of *Corners of the Circle*. I would install a piece in four different churches in the four corners of Belfast: the Church of the Nativity, Catholic Parish in Poleglass, west Belfast; Jennymount Methodist Church in north Belfast; Saint Nicholas' Church of Ireland in south Belfast; and Belmont Presbyterian in east Belfast. Not being sure what each installation was going to be, I set about visiting the clergy and attended a service in each church. This allowed me to work out where the congregation sit and the dynamic of the church.

In conversation with the clergy of the four churches, each one gave me an area in their church the size of a small chapel in which I installed all the paper documents I'd received when attending services. They were threaded together with purple or red ribbons, and once sitting on the pews and seats along with mirrors and photographs of some of the churches it made for an interesting spectacle. Suddenly there was a connection with the sheer amount of variety within churches and the time to sit among the documents and wonder what it's all about.

The pieces were to stay in situ for the duration of the 4 Corners Festival and people were encouraged to sit among the installations for a service – a christening and two confirmations were included. Many thought this was too much of an ask but some people did attend with me, commenting that somehow I was getting something else out of the service. As I sat in the Church of the Nativity for their second confirmation service, with all the children wearing sashes instead of formal dress, my inner being glowed with light and a sharp crystal of knowing formed within my head. I felt privileged to be witnessing it.

On the Saturday of the festival I took several people on a performative bus journey around the churches. It made for an interesting experience. People were asked to arrive at PS² Gallery for refreshments before getting on a bus in front of Saint Anne's Cathedral. Off we went to Jennymount Methodist in north Belfast. On the journey I explained my work in north Belfast and that I was going to ask people to do different things in each church.

We arrived and entered the eight-year-old church (Jennymount Methodist had been completely rebuilt after the boiler had exploded and made the church uninhabitable). Ecclesiastical music was playing and I asked people not to speak. Everyone moved around the church trying to work out where the art piece was. We all sat down, soaking up the atmosphere and connecting to the spirit of the piece and the place. Slowly people realised which bit was the art. After about fifteen minutes we made our way to the next stop. On the bus was a relaxed atmosphere and conversation flowed; great calm infused. I no longer felt in charge as a group support dynamic had happened very quickly and I chatted to Father Martin instead. A pilgrimage spirit was forming and people were getting to know each other.

The next stop was Saint Nicholas' Parish on the Lisburn Road. Someone asked if the bus driver could join us too. "Of course he can," I said. "Art and church are for everyone." As we got off the bus I looked around and realised we were at the wrong church. We were on the Lisburn Road but were a short walk away from Saint Nicholas'. With so many churches on that one road it's easy to get confused. The bus driver apologised and said we were at the church his parents had got married in. Slowly we walked up the Lisburn Road as if towards a light, conscious that here we were slipping into another world when all around people were out for their Saturday shopping. Some of the group met people they knew who tried to take them off in another direction (just like dealing with your spirituality in real life). It felt as if I was leading them towards a light which beckoned us forward as we arrived at Saint Nicholas'. Giving instructions before entering, I asked people to be silent, sign in to the church and then complete a walking meditation around it – my work was installed in a route around the church.

Saint Nicholas' is a more traditional church having been built in 1901. There were classic pews, poppy wreaths on the walls, British Legion banners and a wooden pulpit. At one point I got people to sit in the pews where a lot of the artwork was installed. Music rang out and the atmosphere was thick with energy. Some people started to get very emotional and slowly moved out of the church. Some came to me to say they felt unable to continue. It was as if that day had connected them to the last experience they had had in church. For one man it was his father's funeral; another spoke of how it immediately reminded them of their mother, who had recently died, taking them to church when they were small. People were directly connecting to their last church experience just by the physical act of sitting down in the church. For a couple, I think the thought of going to Poleglass in west Belfast was too much, but off we went with one person seeing some tricolours along the route saying, "Oh, look, we're going to Ireland."

We stopped at the Church of the Nativity on Bell Steel Road – named after Belle Steel, an eighteenth-century Presbyterian. She lived in a cottage in the townland of Poleglass, on the outskirts of Belfast and Lisburn, along what is now Stewartstown Road. Her place in history comes from her sympathy for the Roman Catholic faithful who, under Penal Law, were denied their church buildings for worship. Steel was the trusted custodian of the sacred vessels used in the liturgy, as well as a small horn used to summon the faithful to Mass. She kept watch for soldiers approaching and provided warnings to people attending Mass. There is a stained-glass window dedicated to her inside the church. Some on the bus felt comforted by this – that with all our historic divisions individuals shone through and did what they could.

The atmosphere in this church was again completely different – light and airy in a contemporary setting around eight years old and completely funded by the local parish. A meditative walk around the edges brought us to the full immersion baptismal font, then on to the icon and purple chapel area that held the installation. The priest, the Very Reverend Pat Sheenan, had put up a welcome sign on the overhead projector.

I sat down and a young man came and sat beside me.

"Do you know this is where people sit to wait for confessions?"

I said, "Oh, sorry, I didn't mean to disturb you."

"What do you think about Buddhism?" he asked.

I've been asked this on numerous occasions. It feels as though people are moving away from the tradition they were born into, suddenly thinking there might be something in it after all, and Buddhism is the furthest away from the sectarian religious past that you can get, so why not investigate that? I've great respect for the local Buddhist community and all the different strands, which have a deep richness. I've attended events and retreats and found Buddhists to be people of deep faith and strong practice. I love their calm presence, which is contagious when you're in their company.

I invited Father Martin to talk a bit about his experience of being a priest in the area. He spoke of the work to get the new church built and the amount of suicides he had had to deal with. I thought of the two priests in the parish covering such a large area and compared this to some of the reformed faiths who have very small congregations.

We headed for the last church, Belmont Presbyterian in east Belfast. As we drove down Belmont Road one of the participants said, "Look, there's the church."

"No, not the right one," I said.

"There's another one."

86

This started a good discussion about which church is the right church and how do you know. We arrived at Belmont Presbyterian, signed the visitors' book and made our way to the front. This being our last church, people were getting confused about the signs and symbols different denominations use and wondered what the difference was. As we sat among the pews, we wondered ever more what it was all about.

Tea and coffee were offered as we chatted over our experience. Reverend Jack Lamb, Presbyterian minister at Townsend Street on the Shankill, had accompanied us, and I asked him to talk a bit about Presbyterians. He lightened the atmosphere by saying he wasn't responsible for all Presbyterians to which everyone laughed!

Arriving back at Saint Anne's Cathedral we hugged and chatted before going our separate ways. There was a feeling that we'd been on a pilgrimage. Usually divided into our own sections of Belfast, we had travelled over many barriers to come to a place of integration. I checked in with participants who had left the group early to make sure everyone was okay. People were open about the effect the journey had had on them and thanked me for doing it. As for me, I was on an art high – but just wanted to get home and be fed.

A few participants who had got caught in traffic and missed the tour were annoyed, so I decided to do another piece called *For All Our Ancestors*. Reverend Elizabeth Hanna in Saint Nicholas' Parish Church was delighted to host, and Mick McEvoy a practitioner of Thich Nhat Hanh Zen Buddhism joined me to bring people around a walking meditation inside the church. All the pieces from the other three churches were installed inside Saint Nicholas'.

I arrived late and everyone was already inside walking around the church. Allowing them time to acclimatise, we then invited them to the front of the church where we gave a small introduction before slowly making our way around the route of the church pews we had prepared. We then allowed for a pew stop and sit down for some reflection.

Mick McEvoy then had an opportunity to speak for a while about his walking meditations and mindfulness in general before Reverend Hanna explained more about the church. All attendees that day, adults and children, weren't churchgoers except two, and it offered secular people an opportunity to connect into the spiritual traditions we have here and open a space for thinking and dialogue.

I chose the name *For All Our Ancestors* for the art piece because I felt this needed clarified and understood – that our ancestors have a story to tell and their narratives aren't the same, and that although there must be a way to respect that, we need to ensure that now there is a different reality. A softening of attitude is required as well as a doorway into healing. I would like to develop this further but every day I have new ideas and the difficulty is how to get support to advance them; how to lead this artistic activity without making myself ill or bankrupt or both.

Pondering on the day afterwards, I felt changed, delighted to finally work out how my experiences can be formed into art and interested in people's reactions to the art piece. I can see how clergy and the religious community would benefit from artists as mediators with the secular public, who are quick to point blame and close their ears to many living a religious life. Artists, however, can open up a space for different thinking and dialogue. On entering different denominations people are challenged to let go of previous understanding, or lack of it. Simply crossing a threshold offers a challenge to many; being allowed to experience "the other" in a different way is the key. One participant, Emeritus Professor Pauline Murphy, said, "Stepping into the church felt very cold to me, the symbols of the Church of Ireland being unfamiliar, yet the connection made while there brought me to a very deep feeling of fellowship with all beings."

In 2015 I was at the Community Relations Awards for Civic Leadership. Máirtín Ó Muilleoir MLA, who won the award the year before for his work while Lord Mayor of Belfast, was presenting the award to Linda Ervine who set up the thriving Irish language education strand of East Belfast Mission right in the heart of loyalist east Belfast; both very worthy recipients.

I asked the assembled audience when are we going to stop thinking of community relations as something to make money off or rolling our eyes when it's mentioned. The reaction I received when I started to make my own artwork on the interface: "That's where the money is," not "You must have a deep and compelling desire to process your experiences," as case in point. Such is the evolution of the peace and reconciliation industry.

Speaking to Máirtín afterwards I told him how concerned I was that the EastSide Arts Festival had moved away from the very community it was for, that the artists who had expended their energy getting it off the ground were being marginalised – as they still are.

I found myself walking into a free coffee morning in Saint Martin's on the Newtownards Road a couple of hours later. I didn't know the church had been deconsecrated, but by the time I left that day we'd agreed to take over the church for the festival, curate an exhibition and run a series of events in it. As usual, the financial support we were promised didn't materialise but we decided to do it anyway. Hats off to Reverend John Cunningham and his wife Linda who just welcomed, as they say, "A little bit of light into the darkness."

The church attracted me as it was situated on an interface and was really spacious inside. It had a great walled garden and when I'd been based in the building beside it, I'd often thought what a nice spot it was. My long-time collaborator Suellen came up with the name *Still Bunker* and came over from Chicago to share the experience with me. Under the name of the Hydrangea Project we installed work from ten Belfast artists along with a limited-edition print portfolio from Iraq veterans against the war. Four performance artists were also included on the opening night. Suellen and I had decided on the name Hydrangea project, naming it after the flower we had used in the Lament per formative walk, the idea being that the same flower can grow in different soil and change colour accordingly, just like our project.

Christoff Gillen researched in the area earlier in the week and drew a chalk rainbow down the Newtownards Road from Saint Patrick's Church. The local kids and community helped him, with one person even coming out to give him extra chalk.

The area itself has seen a lot of violence and many people from outside the district didn't even want to walk there, so it was an effort to even get people to attend. We ran a series of events including poet Maria McManus doing Poetry from a Pulpit with ten poets and two musicians, each taking turns in the candlelight to read their own poetry from the existing pulpit. The assembled group felt the importance of the event and buzzed with the energy generated by these simple acts of creativity. Stephen Millar and Nathan Crothers invented a talk show one lunchtime with artists' guests complete with digital title sequence. The local children came every day to see what was happening, and one day we carried a pew outside to enjoy the sun and were joined by the local kids for an interview with Northern Visions Television NVTV, a local cable TV channel.

On the opening night the atmosphere was amazing inside the church, the magical acoustics amplifying artist Jayne Cherry's beautiful voice as people watched transfixed by her performance ensuring that when they entered the exhibition, they gave it the hushed church-like reverence it deserved. Isobel Anderson took them underwater with her audiovisual performance, part of which was listened to blindfolded. I installed the *Corners of the Circle* piece in a square of four pews with a kneeling piece of furniture in the middle strewn with church ephemera. At the end of the evening some people were picking up Bibles and hymn books and asking, "What is this all about anyway?" Other artists included were Brendan O Neill, Rachel Rankin, Frankie Quinn, Caroline McClusker, and Keith Ayton. Rev John Cunningham, who is still minister at the church, says, "I'm not sure how it happened but *Still Bunker* has contributed to the transformed the bottom of the Newtownards Road," and urged us to come back the following year.

Still without support, except for £350, I curated *Still Bunker 2*. This time installing work from Sinead McKeever, Colin Clarke, Alex Connolly, Frankie Xavier Devlin, SeVen, John Baucher, Frankie Quinn, Ellie Niblock, Caroline McClusker, Brendan O'Neill and Stephen Millar's work with Scoil an Droichid. Opening night also had performances from Hugh O'Donnell, Jayne Cherry, Infinity farm and Paul Moore's #nonarnia. Peter Osborne, chair of the Community Relations Council, was christened in the church and I asked him to open the exhibition. Máirtín Ó Muilleoir MLA, who was then finance minister, attended. The result was a bizarre art–church fete with a mix of people from divergent backgrounds of historically opposing sides and different histories wandering around and mixing, making connections, cutting through the traumatised community body and shifted perceptions. Bbeyond Performance artists took over the space the following day and local children were mesmerised, asking what it was. "Do you know the way you can make art with a pencil, well performance art is when you make art with your body," was the reply. Dr Robin Price magicked up an amazing evening of visuals and sounds, while Maria McManus and eleven poets from all over the world who called Belfast home poured out their creativity into the night air.

Outside the police set up a temporary metal wall and filmed with CCTV camera a band parade that was going up the Newtownards Road. "What is this all about?" asked the visitors. What indeed. Personally, we think the traumatised structures that have emerged in Northern Ireland support a militaristic solution – and it's easy to see why, but it's not going to be a military solution that changes the dynamic, that's for sure. Where is the liminal space in between where new conversations and connections are made and are allowed to form? How can artists use their time-honoured skills to help? How have they been helping without support? Is there an energy that manifests when artists simply do that?

In 2017 we returned to the space for *Still Bunker 3*. Our exhibition title was *Liminal*. Ten artists including Frankie Quinn, Siobhan Mullan Wolfe, Zara Lyness, Hugh O Donnell, John Baucher and thirty-two adults with learning difficulties exhibited their work. Bbeyond held one of their performance art monthly's. A series of panel discussions on the art of healing were scheduled and opened a conversation about the transformation of the area. John Kyle PUP councillor for the area has been very supportive. A more cultural dynamic is palpable resulting in many more arts organisations using the building for performances and events. Saint Martin's has become a cultural asset within the community. As pioneers we're not recognised, supported or acknowledged, yet the sweet contentment of artistic achievement fills our hearts and carry on we must. In 2018, asking the Festival organiser why there is no activity in the Short Strand area, on the other side of the peace wall, and not getting a satisfactory answer, we removed ourselves from the festival.

Another piece I did that relates was *Connect*. We decided to perform another walking meditation and happened to pick 5 August, the anniversary of internment, to do it. Internment is the arrest and detention of people without trial or due process. It is often used during periods of war or conflict to remove perceived dangerous individuals from civilian society. Internment was introduced in Northern Ireland by Brian Faulkner, Prime Minister of Northern Ireland, in August 1971, which inflamed tensions, displaced seven thousand people and led to an increase in violence and tensions. Every year the date is marked, in previous years with bonfires and disobedience but in contemporary Belfast with marches and commemoration parades, some still try and have bonfires but there is a call to stop this practice. At the time of *Connect* there was an ongoing contentious dispute about the Ardoyne roundabout in north Belfast. The Orange Order wanted to parade there in July and many locals objected to the route they wanted to take. This led to annual riots and the area acted like a magnet for people wanting to create disturbance at certain times of the year.

Suellen and I invited people to meet us at the roundabout and proceeded to complete a filmed walking meditation similar to that completed in east Belfast the year before. It was very quiet, with only six people joining us, and people said they didn't come because they feared the area. We noticed in particular that locals were suspicious of us giving them flowers and breath poems, but the Indian men working in the takeaways were delighted to have an artistic distraction on their doorstep. It's interesting trying to explain the significance of such an area to an outsider: why was there a caravan with Union Jacks on it? What's all the fuss about? Sometime later the dynamic of the area changed.

On International Women's Day 2014, along with Anne Murphy, a shamanic healer, and Elvina Porter McCullough, we invited people to join us at Buoy Park, in front of Belfast Art College. Anne had completed a shamanic journey to find what ritual we should do. We spent some time completing a performance and meditating before taking up our positions in the Women's Day march. Making our way down Royal Avenue, we were joined by some friends from the States and groups of women. Thousands of women were in the march. Our group carried the energy of our meditation down Royal Avenue with us, trying to lull a rowdy crowd. It was the year that the flag protesters were doing a weekly protest in front of the city hall, and as we walked down Royal Avenue a large group of protesters blocked the road with

Union Jacks. As women have a tendency to do, we separated and passed around them in a non-confrontational flow of women. As we reached the stage Anne and I stood beside a couple with a large Union Jack. The more I rang the bell I'd been carrying since our performance earlier, the stronger the couple stood rooted to the ground in a kind of trance. At one point a group to the left started to get quite aggressive, so we moved over and stood in front of them ringing the bell and trying to hold the energy. They too stood in a kind of daze. After the speeches, which were constantly interrupted by hecklers, we made our way into the city hall for refreshments. I continuously rang the bell; Anne completed a closing performance and Elvina filmed it. After the meditation we contemplated the experience, wondering if our non-violent intervention had contributed in any way to the peaceful passing off of the march.

With Suellen I have witness her deliver art and nonviolence training with Ken Buttigan of Pace e bene to Iraq veterans against the war before they delivered the performative action of throwing their medals back to NATO in downtown Chicago, Suellen was one of the mental health support working on the march insuring veterans would not be led into violence while marching. Together we supported a veteran retreat in Blue Cliff monastery New York using art, mindfulness and body work techniques with other professionals to try and bring veterans that have a very high suicide rate in the states further along their path to healing. We have tried to develop the connection between Belfast and Chicago, further connecting the two cities as we believe the work around shifting veterans from Iraq, Afghanistan and Vietnam out of violence using art and complementary techniques has useful learning for the Northern Ireland experience. At this point we have been unsuccessful in gaining substantial support for this work despite lobbying as there is currently no mechanism or understanding of what we are talking about or importance the artist's role within it. In fairness Northern Ireland Action for Mental health now called Inspire tried to support us on two occasions but I think the inherent suspicion and lack of understand of how the freedom of the artist and curatorial decisions are important is part of the issue. We believe we have developed a contemporary art practice underpinned with art therapy that acts as a healing mechanism within contentious space, left behind by conflict and wish only to develop it further for wider benefit.

Chapter 17: Take a Pew

It's been a rarity to attend a church with standing room only. These services have usually been at Catholic churches for special occasions, Easter or at Clonard Novena where over twenty thousand people attend multiple services in the run-up to summer solstice – nothing to do with the comfort of the seats! Sometimes this overspill disappears and people leave early once Communion has been taken.

There's a large selection of options for seating arrangements in churches, pews being only one of them. Fixed seats weren't often seen in churches before the Reformation. Pew renting was stopped in the 1940s; in the Church of Ireland it was tradition to rent your pew for the year to raise income for the church. Pews were originally made of plane wood but a wide variety have evolved to bring more comfort to the proceedings.

In some churches the territorial seating arrangements have allowed for cushions more accustomed to a sofa (left behind for the comfort of repeat churchgoers). In others, a flat cushion or strips of carpet keep the hardness at bay. Some seats have evolved with the age of the congregation who have installed more cushioned, comfortable seating as their bones grew weary. Calvary Baptist is one church that has modernised its seating, moving from traditional pews to soft chairs, as it simply wanted to make it more comfortable for their congregants. I've even seen armchairs with winged sides provided for the comfort of the congregation in a small gospel hall in north Belfast, ensuring a homely atmosphere for anyone requiring it. "I like going to Catholic services," said a friend brought up in the Methodist tradition. "Catholics don't mind getting down on their knees to pray and are quicker to do so," which means kneelers are much more readily available. It made me smile when reading about the refurbishment of Saint Bernadette's off Knock Dual Carriageway, with its beautiful Elizabeth Frink crucifixion sculpture hanging over the altar. I was reading on their website that their refurbishment included seating, but after arriving for a Mass I realised that only the long wooden kneelers had cushioning, not the seats – so you can kneel in comfort but not sit!

Some churches have informal cafe-style seating arrangements: Redeemer Central and City Church in Botanic being two of these. At City Church I attended their very informal family church service. Families new to the church would find circular tables filled with art aids to the service circled by chairs very welcoming. There's no need to worry about children not sitting quietly to listen to the service – although when I visited, I heard one church member say "I'm just too old for this."

At the beginning of my church attendance I was very aware of seating arrangements and not wanting to take anyone's seat. I thought that all churches have territorial congregations, but soon found there was enough space for everyone. It's only been on a very rare occasion I've been asked to move. Once an elderly woman said to me, "Do you not notice the name on the Bible in front of you? That's Bobby's seat," at which moment an elderly gentleman in a suit came to claim the space even though there were forty empty spaces around him. Another time I was told, "That's my husband you're sitting beside," and was rather indignantly asked to move. Once more I was apologised to as a husband swapped seats with his wife. She said, "I'm sorry, my husband's not really used to new people. His parents didn't have many people visiting their house." Thinking I could sit anywhere I wanted on arrival turned into handbags on seats – "That's taken!" – when I went to sit down. But this is rare. In general, there's much less territory claiming than I had imagined. Congregations are delighted to welcome people into their worship space. It was really my own memory of churchgoing as a child that I had been thinking of when everyone always sat in the same place and rarely there was a visitor to a service.

Every time I'm in a Presbyterian church, in all their varieties, on being identified as a new face someone will come and sit beside me and welcome me to the service. I've had some really interesting conversations this way; talking about the history of the church, the ministers, times the church was bombed – it never seems invasive.

Once in a Baptist church, an elderly woman tried to wedge me at the end of the pew using her handbag so that she could do a recruitment drive on me. I've since noticed that that small congregation has moved and a more contemporary-marketed church has taken up residence.

In the first Elim church I attended, on the Newtownards Road, I got a bit of a surprise. When I entered there were several older women and people from the Roma community. One woman came to sit beside me and asked if that was okay. Then the service started and the woman transformed into a jumping-up-and-down-flag-waving-euphoric member of the congregation. She suddenly stood up at one stage and recited a Bible passage. It startled me a bit, but she seemed so happy to have done it. At the end of the service she apologised and said, "I knew I would get something if I sat beside you," sure that my presence had contributed to her inspired Bible reading.

Coming down the Falls Road in west Belfast around the time of Clonard Novena, I wandered into one of the services. Finding it full, I sat in one of the perpendicular pews at the side, more useful for waiting for confessions than taking a service. Coming to the part of the service where a collection was taken, a young woman gave me a collection basket and asked me to do one section of the congregation. I had to ask twice which area she was talking about, but then proceeded to hand it to each row, successful in my first ever church collection. I smiled, wondering what my grandmother would have thought.

I found I enjoyed soaking up the atmosphere before a service when the last preparations were underway. "Be still and know that I am here" became more than a wall hanging at Christmas 2018, and I notice Clonard Monastery is offering more than spiritual comfort by upholstering some of its pews.

"Is there anyone sitting here?" the woman asked. It had happened again. Walking into the church I was welcomed by a number of people at the doorway who smiled and shook hands with me. I took the Bible and hymn book offered and found a seat. In many churches at least one if not two or three people will come and welcome you to their church; however, in Catholic churches it has been my experience that no one ever speaks to you as a stranger. Once in Saint Malachy's a woman commented that I hadn't blessed myself, and another time in Donegal when coming in late to a service a woman said under her breath, "You have a bit of a cheek thinking you can say you went to Mass when you missed the start." Once a conversation started with a man in the church car park about the confirmation service we had just attended. The priest had made everyone laugh when a child had said her mum and dad didn't make her say her prayers before bed. He said, "You must be very deprived!" A colleague working in the arts told me that when she moved house to a new area, it took three years of attending a well-to-do Catholic church before anyone spoke to her.

The reason given to me for this connection, or lack of it, is that in most churches that aren't Catholic it's someone's job to identify any new faces and welcome them. I'm struck by how much commonality the churchgoers of any denomination have over the secular world outside. Whether they speak to me or not, each congregation around the city is fighting off a secular malaise that's happening on the outside. The malaise doesn't seem as strong in Northern Ireland as it is in other parts of the UK and Ireland, but relevant all the same, pulsing through our media and their daily output around and about us. But how can people be encouraged to see what I've seen and experienced – an alternative view of the spiritual life of the city? It's not, I think, about updating the Bible, as one person asked me, "How are the Prods getting on? Still plenty of people going to church? That's great, but what they need to do is update the Bible and add cars and technology."

Chapter 18: Who Gets to Talk in Church?

I didn't really understand gender inequality until sometime into my twenties. I always thought it passé – something that was left behind with burning bras and the sixties; however, being brought up in a household of four girls by my mother on her own, I was acutely aware that women were often left to deal with the aftermath of a relationship breakdown and usually ended up pulling more than half their weight in a given situation.

When I was running women's development programmes it was my connection with the Training for Women Network, and in particular Professor Pauline Murphy, that started to give me an understanding of gender inequality from a research perspective. What were the statistical realities of women's lives?

In my years as a member of the Women's Coalition I benefited from being around strong women who made an impact, who brought a different perspective to the peace talks and used their skills to further peace. I ran cross border women's development programmes and used to deliver gender awareness training I am deeply aware of contemporary gender politics, so it was with these lenses and awareness that I crossed the thresholds of the churches.

On a basic level I observed what women were doing in each of the churches – we are over fifty per cent of the population after all, but is this mirrored by our positions in church? There are certain denominations that echo the gender politics of when they were founded. Without going into history or herstory about it, women's positions have been very much regulated over the years. How is this reflected in contemporary churches?

Listening. There is no doubt that although many denominations have women clergy, the majority of congregations spend their time listening to men. This is just how it is. There are some amazing men out there leading churches – too many to mention. Superintendent David Campton of the Agāpé Centre requires special mention for his epic sermon on sex; the only man brave enough to tackle the subject head-on with such finesse, much to the great amusement of the congregation.

It seems that there are many more women than men going to church on a regular basis. This, I think, is more pronounced in the Catholic Church were in some areas few men attend Mass, particularly teenage boys – at least that's my perception. The women in these churches do, however, seem very active in running the parishes themselves. Grandmothers play an important role and are very active in the city bringing their grandchildren to church.

Even when there is no central administration and years of studying to become clergy, the female parishioners often conform to the position of listener, not the listened to; as in the instance of the gospel halls where I've never heard a woman speak or lead a hymn. In Presbyterian churches when I've heard trainee ministers speak the gospel, they are always young men. They may read scripture like a rap or hold court about a Bible verse with all their charisma but the young women are the ones sitting down taking notes, not leaning from the front. Why? In some of the churches that simply call themselves Christian like CFC or Re: Hope women can lead the services but they are usually married. The Salvation army tend to put couples in charge of their churches and I've enjoyed a service where a toddler has run up to its mum's arms while she has delivered a service. Much to the joy of the congregation.

Female ministers bring an added dimension to proceedings. There is a feminine presence and usually a softness to their delivery. For some people who have specific issues with how they received religious instruction in the past, attending a church with a woman minister could be a way back into faith. I believe you can visually compare a life with God to a life outside God by looking into a woman minister's eyes. Compare the gaze to that of a woman of comparable age who doesn't have a practicing faith. The difference is palpable. Controversially I believe it's the same with women in the congregation; there is more of an embodied spiritual presence shining out from their eyes that is very different from the ones you see in secular life – deadened eyes with hardened demands, women, young and old, hardened by life.

Think about how church services are designed, and then think about who actually gets to speak. My first time in a Quaker service, I joined the congregation sitting in a square and after a period of silence whoever felt moved by the spirit to speak stood up and gave the teaching of the week. The idea is that you think about the teaching during the week and reply the following Sunday. Men and women can both speak – how radical this must have been mid-seventeenth century when they started. Considering that in some churches women still don't speak, what are the implications of this? The silence held in the Quaker service is recognisable to anyone used to meditation. Stilling the mind. "Be still and know that I am God". I found the silence welcoming, similar to that in some gospel halls. I had a very interesting conversation with a woman after the service. She was originally from North Down but had lived in London for a long time. On returning to the province she went to a few different churches but felt uninspired before someone told her about the Quakers. After attending one of their services, she was hooked.

I'm thinking of possible reactions or what would have happened if some other denominations in Northern Ireland practised the same form of service. What of child abuse, fraud, institutional abuse and sexual misconduct within churches – topics that have repeatedly grabbed the headlines over the last number of years? What if any congregant could stand up and talk in a service – what would the impact have been? Quakers don't have any minister or priest professing the priesthood of all believers, which puts more onus on the individual. It's interesting how different radical notions were adopted or suppressed at times – maybe more to do with who owns the land and buildings, and fear over losing them, than anything else.

Quakers are known for their non-violent stance, and in particular in the past in Northern Ireland for prisoner-family services in prisons. They do still work in prisons. They also operated a Quaker house for peacemaking for twenty-eight years on Black Mountain. The house is still there but acknowledging that although there is still a need for peacemaking, the Quaker house is "no longer an appropriate vehicle for this work" it closed in 2010.

It's interesting to think of how gender segregation has developed in different religious strands and the effect on the life of the spirit as a result; whether it be different sides of the church to sit on for services, different parts of the graveyard to be buried in or men only being allowed to lead services.

Women clergy were a marvellous find. The Church of Ireland voted to allow women clergy in 1990 and had its first female bishop in 2013. The Presbyterian church voted woman in forty years ago and the different Methodist stands have varying stances in allowing women clergy. Denominations that allow women clergy have increased the catchment for church vocations from the fifty-one per cent of the population that are women. At a time when clergy vocations have dropped, this has allowed many denominations to be saved. Sometimes when I attend Catholic services and look at the female Eucharist ministers, I think that some of them could minister if they belonged to one of the Protestant reformed denominations as they have the same spiritual aura around them. But will it ever happen? Well, suffice to say a female minister told me that when she was invited to do part of the service at Clonard Novena a woman came up to her afterwards and said she couldn't wait for women priests in the Catholic Church, but she felt she would be waiting a long time.

I find many female clergy inspiring and welcomed by their congregations, but that's not to say that they've been accepted with ease all around. Coming out of one Presbyterian church when a woman took the service, I heard an older man mutter under his breath, "It feels like I'm being told off by a schoolteacher when she takes the service," so universal acceptance is not there yet.

In smaller gospel halls and Brethren meetings I've never heard women speak, only sing, but there can be a more freestyle service with different people taking turns to read from the Bible. It's never the women who do it, although they do request hymns in this way, giving a certain freedom. There are, however, some services where hymns are requested from the congregation in real time, such as Malvern Assembly in the Shankill area. Here I've found women standing up and requesting hymns freely. It's a kind of hymn karaoke that keeps everyone on their toes. It's pretty unique in the city and quite spectacular. They also work a lot with autistic youth.

While thinking about where gender sits in the church, it was suggested to me that the Catholic Church is more feminine in nature – being able to widen out its scope to include new movements within the church family and integrating them under a wide umbrella – but the Protestant Church is more male in nature, cutting off from each other and starting new denominations when disagreements occur. Patriarchy at its best – or worst, perhaps. Is it all about entitlement? After all a precedent was set.

Speaking in tongues is explained as the Holy Spirit speaking through individuals, even though it might sound like gibberish to the listeners. On the three occasions I've experienced it in church, two have been by women and one by a male pastor. It seemed to me, as an observer, that each individual reached peak Holy Spirit and then this vocabulary took over as if from another dimension. The pastor started it as he was in a sermon. It was very eloquent and quite interesting to listen to.

In 2017 at the 4 Corners Festival I heard a priest say that we don't know if God is a man or a woman, and everyone laughed. But what exactly is it we're unpicking? It seems to me that some people who hold issue with male clergy could be encouraged to look at faith differently simply by joining a church with a female minister. Reverend Ruth Patterson sticks out in my mind as a good example, as do Reverend Heather Bell and Reverend Elizabeth Hanna, now retired. Reverend Karen Sethuraman has an interesting ministry with the Down community. A female Baptist minister endorsed by the Great Britain Baptists but not the Irish ones, she has cut a space for herself in developing an outreach role to gather people who she helps figure out their relationship to God and then encourages them into different denominations depending on how their faith develops. I first came across Karen in 2017 when she was on a panel at the 4 Corners Festival. In the intervening years Karen has moved into north Belfast SoulSpace along with Gordon McDade, connected to 174 Trust, and became one of Councillor Deirdre Hargey's Sinn Fein's chaplains when she was Lord Mayor of Belfast. We wait to see what unfolds. The time I attended her gathering there was an interesting group of people some from the LGBTQ community and various others who hadn't yet found a place to develop their spirituality; some weren't even sure if they had one.

There is something about the invisibility of a woman in her fifties that allows me to be unobtrusive, ignored even, although sometimes suspicions are raised. The times I brought my husband to church felt different. Even though he was brought up as a French Catholic he was

confused by Presbyterians and asked me if it was an American thing –
"What do you mean you don't have to sit through it all? The kids go
out during the service!". The only service I have attended with a
group of nuns is in the Chapel of perpetual adoration on the Falls
Road but it's a male Priest that leads the service.

If I was younger, I think I'd have had a different reaction. Once a
woman in a gospel hall got annoyed with me and asked if I was
joining the group. I think she was the only unmarried woman there
and saw me as competition for the single men in the group. Another
lady in the same group said she had noticed that the men enjoyed
seeing me there. The odd time someone asked if I was married. Even
the fact of being an artist brought suspicion veiled as interest – what is
your role? Where is the box I can put you in? Where do you belong?

The oldest women I sat beside in a congregation was 106 years
old on the Donegal Road, sometimes I feel for the elderly women in
congregations having no influence or say in wider church matters the
women who when I commented that I thought I needed new glasses to
read their hymn books said "I always thought we just needed books in
larger type" she replied. Has her opinion ever been sought I thought?
How many years had she been thinking that, with no one to listen to
her? When ministers or Pastors are sick, it's always a man in the
congregation that stands in, or a younger man comes from elsewhere
to take the service. Never a young woman.

On the island of Iona on the west coast of Scotland I observed
that the priory that once held monks has been restored but the nunnery
still lies in ruins, the Sheela na gig carved in stone on its walls. When
I attended a service at the priory a woman taking the service
explained "to those who care about such things" that she was an
Anglican priest, and as she led the Communion service, I felt that this
was the leap that women have experienced in more recent times.
Maybe there's no longer a need for the nunnery to be rebuilt as the
women priests are inside taking the service.

Chapter 19: Music, Singing and Dancing in Churches

Music is an art form that churches tend to do well. The variety of music and song within churches is as abundant as the selection of churches themselves. In the Catholic churches in Belfast generally a choir or soloist sing – in marked contrast to the Catholic churches I've attended in the United States where the whole congregation sings.

A friend of mine's introduction to Protestantism was flicking *Songs of Praise* on the TV by mistake before quickly changing channel with embarrassment at what on earth they were doing singing.

There have only been five occasions when I've experienced singing in a Catholic church: Novena in Clonard Monastery, Belfast; Saint Anne's Parish in Dunmurry; twelve o'clock Mass at the Chapel of Perpetual Adoration, Falls Road; Saint Michael The Archangel, Andersonstown, when the priest encouraged the congregation to sing; and in Saint Vincent De Paul Parish, Ligoniel, when a confirmation was in progress and the assembled children replied to the priest in song.

Investigating why this might be the case I came across the book *Why Catholics Can't Sing* by Thomas Day. Years later this could still be the reason Catholic congregations don't generally sing:

> The Irish people were persecuted for centuries. Their glory is that they "kept the faith". There was little opportunity for singing at Masses celebrated behind the hedge rows; one did not have to attract the attention of English soldiers by singing. The silent low Mass was the norm.

I've found that one part of the service I really like is the singing. When it doesn't happen, for me there is a feeling of an opportunity missed. The simple feel-good factor I get from singing as part of a group is absent. Jill Purce, a pioneer of sound healing, states:

> The joy of communal hymn singing is that it not only vibrates the whole system like a sonic massage but transcends the

boundaries that separate us, so singing together in unison we become as one. Nothing else does that.

Wonderful choirs are to be found all over Belfast – some small, others much larger, but all dedicated week after week to bringing an extra dimension to church services. Several choirs release their own CDs, particularly around Christmas, notably Saint Peter's Cathedral with Schola Cantorum and Saint Polycarp's and the Finaghy Choral Society. Some choirs, however, are in steep decline with determined choristers, complete with robes, in groups of ones and twos sitting in the choir pews evoking a formerly much larger group.

An interesting development that can be heard in Ballyculter Parish Church is recorded hymns. With only a small congregation, a recording of both the music and singing are heard, which gives congregants the confidence not to feel so self-conscious about singing themselves. Digital projectors are popular in many churches and playing organ music from you tube videos is an interesting way to get over a lack of live music.

My renewed love of singing has brought me to join a choir myself – the NewQuay Singers connected to Portico in Portaferry; a Presbyterian meeting house converted into a cultural centre that still has a congregation connected to it. We practise in Holywood, then congregate in Portico, Portaferry, for carols, requiems and harvest thanksgiving. As this is the time of year I'm visiting, it's convenient to attend.

The choir consists of people who normally sing in their local churches all over County Down but who come together for the challenge of trying new music and being part of something bigger. Professional soloists are sometimes linked in for performances and as a singer I've noticed during practice or performances the feeling of combined spiritual energy can be simply amazing. Neil McClure runs the choir and interestingly for me the energy changes depending on the music sung. Requiems in particular seem to generate a deep swirling energy. Sometimes. it feels to me like a starburst coming from the inside of my being; or fluttering on the inside and outside the energy is amplified by being together. Pretty amazing.

I've only experienced one traditional Irish group in church – it was in a service at Clonard Monastery, but other bands have had every type of instrument included in their set-up. Guitars are popular, both electric and acoustic, but full drum kits can be quite the norm along with bongos, flutes, saxophones, bodhráns and trumpets – and I found a magical violinist in Ballybeen. Often these more contemporary ensembles can be found in the absence of a piano or an organ, but other times they play alongside. In Baptist churches I've experienced men in their Sunday best suits turn into rock stars as soon as the music starts – lighting up from the inside – as they lead the band.

The Salvation Army must have the largest church band in Belfast. I counted over thirty instruments – every imaginable brass instrument and drum accompaniment – in Belfast Temple on the Cregagh Road when I visited them for their one hundred and thirty-fifth anniversary. Other churches rely on no accompaniment, the communal purity of the a cappella singing harking out. I enjoy it when I'm unsure as to who might be the musician, then watch as they connect with their instruments. A woman in her later years with headphones behind a drum kit is a delight to watch.

Many of the more evangelical churches play around two or three hymns at the beginning of the service, one after the other. This practice raises the spirits of the congregation immediately – or can make you feel like you're starring in a musical. Dundonald Elim is well known for this, but with the request to stand as well it can sometimes make me feel lightheaded.

In some churches hymn books are no longer used as overhead projectors dominate and ensure continuity of verse singing. Only rarely does the sync of the projection not match the verses being sung, which can make the congregation giggle and the person in charge of audiovisuals fluster. This, however, is the exception and not the norm.

The dedication of the voluntary music teams in churches shouldn't be underestimated. Week after week, year after year, the musical talents of Belfast's congregations support and enhance the worship experience and offer the opportunity to share talents for the betterment of the wider community. It's great to have the surprise of a jazzy keyboard player in a more traditional church or a suited and booted man in his sixties playing a bodhrán in a Baptist church. Anything goes and all musical boundaries are crossed.

On the matter of grace and singing, when Van Morrison received the freedom of Belfast and played a celebration concert at the Waterfront Hall, I stood in the middle of the ground floor at the front of the assembled citizens of Belfast. As he played his saxophone, I felt the grace that flowed from him as he played to the crowd – a physical manifestation of an unseen esoteric world?

Late one summer I came across a congregation in Tullymore Forest having an outdoor Sunday service and singing hymns into the sunshine. Against a mountainous backdrop, I felt the energy that the group was emanating. As I joined them for a hymn, I felt directly linked to the Holy Spirit among them.

Dance is rarer. Irish dancing on Saint Patrick's Day in Clonard Monastery and Down Cathedral is quite beautiful; however, in Chicago I experienced liturgical dance, can be described as:

> "A type of dance movement sometimes incorporated into liturgies or worship services as an expression of worship. The dancers will respond with an appropriate dance which flows out of the music and is thought to enhance the prayer or worship experience."

The dance consisted of over thirty minutes of African-American women and a man dancing in specially designed robes as part of the service. On the particular day I was there, the Catholic service was for Mother's Day and included a sermon from a female Baptist preacher (not likely to happen in Northern Ireland) who stirred the congregation with wisdom from her mother; sage advice including if you lie down with dogs you get up with fleas. Two hours into the service we had to leave for another meeting, only to be told that the lively service could last as long as three and a half hours! It was designed to help bring the Holy Spirit into the gang neighbourhood to help people survive the week and improve their resilience. That particular church had a number of ministries that did outreach in the wider community, including a manicure ministry. On their notice board outside there were pictures of young people from the area who had died because of gang violence.

To actually experience dancing in the congregation in Belfast I attended the UCKG or Universal Church of the Kingdom of God, which originated in Brazil, a church in inner east Belfast. Some of the songs sang at their Sunday services encourage the congregation to take part in a South American group dance to the words of "Where do you find God?". The multicultural congregation love it and it felt very culturally appropriate for this denomination. There can be a lot of hand waving and swaying in some of the evangelical churches which could be interpreted as dance in another setting.

In getting feedback for this book one person with a strong faith told me of a discussion in their church about whether this evangelical feeling of being uplifted really worked for people. Faith for them was the rock and foundation of everything they did that they took everywhere. My feeling was that at this stage of human development there is more need for people to connect with the reality that God exists than to split hairs over how they might do it; that Northern Ireland, and Belfast in particular, might have something very specific to share with the world, something hidden in plain sight; that some people of faith could afford to be a little more generous to others walking a similar path even if it's in a slightly different way.

Chapter 20: The Physical Nature of Prayer

I once heard Archbishop Justin Welby say that although not quite sure how it works, every revival starts with people praying, and the more praying the more the connection with God develops.

One of my neighbours asked me to talk to the local branch of the Mothers' Union, a Christian organisation connected to the Church of Ireland with more than three and a half million members in seventy-nine countries worldwide, about some of the projects I'd been involved in. The evening started with the Mothers' Union prayer:

> Loving Lord, we thank you for your love so freely given to us all. We pray for families around the world. Bless the work of the Mothers' Union as we seek to share your love through the encouragement, strengthening and support of marriage and family life. Empowered by your Spirit, may we be united in prayer and worship, and in love and service reach out as your hands across the world. In Jesus' name. Amen.

Most of the members were over sixty, many over eighty, and as they spoke the words of the prayer out into the evening air, I could feel the trickle wash over my face. What I mean by this is that it felt like a physical manifestation of the prayer was being launched into the world by these faithful women who had created an energy within themselves and with each other after a lifetime of faith. I read some time later that there was an all-Ireland Mothers' Union conference in the Waterfront Hall and I couldn't help wondering what it would feel like to sit among them while they prayed.

During my talk I started with my early work in England and the United States. I could see eyes glazing over until I started to talk about visiting the church services and then I felt an upsurge in interest. The women appeared to have a kind of glow around them, and as I continued to talk it felt as if a large collective sigh was being held by everyone there – like they were revelling in the bizarre nature of what I was doing, connected by a feeling of relief that perhaps something could be done, wrapped around the issue of religion, about the state of our province.

It was with these experiences that I came to understand that every spiritual practice, if practised over a long enough period of time, must develop subtle energy bodies in different ways. The thought came to me when I was looking at Buddhism, where different strands have a set of spiritual practices to develop an inner Buddha, or Christ consciousness. In Hinduism the Sri Sri Paramahansa Yogananda book *The Second Coming of Christ* talks about the resurrection of the Christ within you. The idea being that if you do certain things over and over it has an effect on your level of consciousness and connection to Christ's consciousness. Taken the other way, if your practice is to go to the pub every day, it will also have an effect on you. Some energy bodies of people are hardened and round, others are softer and more dispersed. Am I seeing the process of sanctification in real time?

In Elim churches their faith seems to develop a soft, subtle energy among the congregation. Before starting this church-attending odyssey I would have crossed the road to avoid a street preacher, but when I noticed one yesterday handing out leaflets and singing a hymn on the street I didn't. His subtle body was highly developed, hardened, rounded with particular emphasis around the head. A teenager walked past taking the leaflet and said, "Anyone want a leaflet? It's just a leaflet." There's some learning there about target markets, but I could see the man was filled with the spirit and wanted to share that experience, which is how I view anyone standing out on the street giving religious literature or preaching, although some say it's brainwashing.

Maybe you too can feel this difference over time with your own practice or faith. I simply became very sensitive to it because of the different paces I was putting my own spirit through. In fact, it was these energetic effects that drew me into exploring church services in the first place. What do I mean by subtle energy bodies? Maureen Lockhart, in her book *The Subtle Energy Body: The Complete Guide* says:

> *"The subtle body is an energetic, psychospiritual entity of several layers or sheaths of increasing subtlety and*

metaphysical significance, through which the aspirant seeks knowledge of the self and the nature of God."

What seemed to be happening to me was that the state of my subtle body was sufficiently developed before my churchgoing, and as I experienced more and more services these energy bodies developed further, making me so sensitive that I quickly picked up the spiritual vibe of anyone around. People also felt it off me. I've often been somewhere when I turn to find someone I don't know standing beside me smiling, convinced that they know me from somewhere even though we've never met before. They are just feeling the vibe but it can be unnerving.

Sometimes when I connect with a church congregation, my whole energy body ignites. It's as if I can directly feel a spiritual stream link with me. A very strong instance of this happened when attending the Gaelic Psalm Singers at Skainos in east Belfast. Linda Ervine had invited the group, who live off the coast of Scotland and sing psalms in Scots Gaelic as part of their spiritual practice, over for the 4 Corners Festival in 2015. They were like nothing I'd ever heard before. A soon as they started singing it was as if my whole energy body electrified. Another time this happened was when I attended an event on mindfulness that Bridgeen Rea-Kaya had organised – a sister of Thich Nhat Hanh monastic traditions from Plum Village monastery did a talk in Belfast before holding a retreat in Corrymeela. Then, I felt a star drop as if from my inner eye to my middle body. Looking into this further I considered the idea that people who have been practising their spirituality in a certain way for generations are like a storehouse for that particular stream of spirituality, and when they come into contact with others, they transfer some of that particular stream. The word "entrainment" also came to mind: the act of taking on a higher level of consciousness while in the presence of a higher-level being.

In three Catholic services – Saint Bernadette's, Saint Agnes' and Saint Mary's lunchtime service, after Mass a group of people stay behind and say the rosary together, sometimes rocking as they talk, taking it in terms to start each prayer and act as the leader. While sitting among them I saw their embodied human presence and felt the power of the prayer streams flow around me. It was Christmas in Saint Peter's for Midnight Mass that I experienced what seemed to be the igniting of my inner eye. It was the first time I'd felt this tingling sensation that lasted for days, almost like a permanent presence, as long as I didn't go near Times Square in New York.

Not being an avid TV watcher, sometimes I catch a glimpse of a TV programme and wonder what's going on in the world. I was in Portaferry looking after my father when I clicked on the TV to watch the news. It was showing a debate in Belfast City Council's chamber about taking down the Union Jack flag over the city hall. The Lord Mayor at the time, Gavin Robinson, DUP, sat like a king at the top of the council, and as I looked and listened it had more of a feeling of a war council than anything else with lots of aggressive male energy. The flag protests followed when some citizens decided to protest by blocking the roads on a daily basis. Shops were losing custom at their busy Christmas trading period, people stopped going out in the evening, except of course the artists. It was a scary time when there was no high-level public leadership to deal with it. Many people were worn down by the protests but felt powerless.

There was one action, however, that showed leadership and hope against a stream of annoyance and inaction: there was to be a prayer circle organised by 24-7 prayer around the city hall one morning at eight o'clock. Unsure if I would attend, I jumped out of bed on the morning in question and drove to the city hall. I joined the circle at the back left-hand side of the city hall and stood with many others, connecting around the circumference of the city hall for five minutes of prayer, trying to bring some positive energy to the city. As the prayers were said I felt an enormous burst of energy flow from my heart – my own prayers amplified by those around me. It was as if the circle of prayer physically manifested itself. When it was over the woman to my left hugged me with a tear in her eye and said, "I know", before we headed off into the Saturday Christmas shopping crowd. Walking around the city hall afterwards to see who turned up, I recognised many of the clergy assembled. People of all ages had heard the call and brought their positivity with them. I was glad of the opportunity to be involved in something hopeful and thought about the physical feeling that the communal prayer evoked. Gavin Robinson DUP was Lord Mayor at the time and he was there without his chain of office and I thought I heard him say, "There are some things that everyone bows down to."

The following week there was a "make noise for peace rally". As I looked around at who had turned up at the front of the city hall, I commented to someone that I'd been there the week before and what a different crowd of people it was that day – a diverse bunch making noise in their own way unlike the well-organised, quiet circle the week before. Someone quickly snapped, "Yes, well, Christians are always used to being told what to do." What a very narrow view that person had and how easily the secular world snaps at the world of people of faith.

After months of demonstrations and disruption, the protests ground to a halt. I had many conversations around that time about the protests, and while some were just embarrassed by it all, at least people were talking about it instead of just thinking it was all going to disappear. Exasperation can be a call to action.

I attended an East Belfast Mission service at Skainos on the Newtownards Road. Here was a congregation much depleted by the protests, in the heart of a community involved with them. Anguish filled the air. As they organised evenings around the streets in prayer groups to do what they could to bring order to the situation, I was aware that in the eyes of many these people were supposed to be the ones protesting, when in reality they were trying to support each other through the nightly protests and do what they could to get them to stop. The strain was evident, and I could feel the sadness and pain in the air of the sanctuary. So much so that it inspired me to write publicly for the first time about what I was witnessing in the church and I sent a mail-out to my community website, feeling compelled to share with people what I had witnessed that no one in the media was talking about. I felt reticent about writing it, knowing that as an artist I was exploring something but unsure how it would manifest in the end. Several people replied to my emails thanking me for what I had written. They had felt a bit isolated and my story had the effect of linking them back into society.

Later, during the 4 Corners Festival, I came across an event called "Listening to your Enemies". Patrick Magee, one of the Brighton Bombers, and Jo Berry, the daughter of a man who died in

114

the bomb attack, were discussing how they became friends. They said they would continue to repeat the sessions anywhere people found them helpful until they stopped being asked. Off I went to Skainos, not knowing there would be a protest outside, and I found myself standing among the men who, twenty minutes before, had made a run for the front doors of the church complex in riot mode. As I stood among them all I could feel was pain. My heart felt like it had so much pain to deal with just by standing among them. The riot police were blocking the entrance, and the assembled men were talking about how much money the riot police got a night and whether it would it pay their phone bills – one had just received a bill and didn't know where the money was coming from to pay it. Jo Berry was reported in a newspaper as saying that she'd been more scared that night than in Bosnia. I was standing outside and didn't feel that at all. I simply felt the pain.

Chapter 21: Do You Ever Want to Go to the Same Church Twice?

Is there any church I've been back to more than once? Of course! There's a number of them. It's always for different reasons – bringing someone else along, seeing if it's the same a second time, curiosity about how they run Easter or Christmas services; however, there are a couple I go back to again and again purely for the energetic experience. One such service is Saint Anne's Cathedral Interdenominational Divine Healing service at 1 p.m. every Friday. It runs for thirty to forty minutes and there's something about it that keeps bringing me back.

I'd heard about the Divine Healing Ministry, founded by Brother David Jardine in 1992 and connected to the Church of Ireland. Interdenominational in nature, it's available across five different locations. People can even send in a prayer request online. The ministry offers one-to-one appointments as well as the lunchtime and evening opportunities for prayer – sometimes wrapped around a service, sometimes not.

Then I found myself sitting beside Reverend Pat Mollan at a Northern Ireland Action for Mental Health event. Reverend Pat works in the ministry and we had a chat about what I was doing. I went to see Pat to ask what she thought about the energetic experiences I was having. We talked about my experience of working in interface areas and the crazy nature of the experience with the physical barriers between people. "Maybe God's plan for Northern Ireland isn't over yet," she said, which made me burst into tears. Pat asked if I wanted her to say a prayer at the end of the session, and as she put her hands on my shoulders, I felt a great surge of energy flowing through my body.

A few weeks later I found myself in the Cathedral Quarter on a Friday lunchtime and decided to join the service. It's held in the small Chapel of the Holy Spirit at the top-right corner of the cathedral. As I walked through the glass doors, I immediately felt a surge of energy and an expansion of spirit.

The service has a different minister every week, rotating reverends from all over Ireland, and it consists of a couple of hymns, the collect, prayers, a sermon on healing and an opportunity for hands-on healing and anointing by five or six people, including the visiting minister. The first time I attended I didn't go up for healing but watched as people of all ages got down on their knees at the rail "in simple faith" and spoke of what they needed healing for – either themselves or by proxy.

One of the healers came to me afterwards and asked if there was anything else I wanted to know. I left with a great sense of expanded consciousness and calm, but was hardly able to ride my bike. The next time I attended, a few weeks later, I went up to the rail and asked that they pray for my father who was suffering from dementia. As the woman hovered her hands over my head, I felt a great rush of energy flow down from above directly into my body. She asked that prayers be said for the wider family and as she said that I felt a widening out of energy and almost a giddy sense of connection. Since then I've went back for myself, family members and friends and observed as people come and connect to the simple service yet leave refreshed. Sometimes the energy is so strong that I don't even have to go up to receive the feeling and just sit quietly as the healing goes on. I've introduced people to it who have found a great sense of clearing with it – the simple touch of a concerned human's hands, the singing of a hymn in the afternoon – as if the dross of the week is cleared off and some level of purity can return to your person.

There is also something about it being a weekday lunchtime. I find it interesting to see who attends church services during the week. They are usually a dedicated and devoted lot using up their lunch hour or spending the early morning in quiet devotion; quite different from the congregation you find at a Christmas carol service or a christening. Their energetic bodies vibrate on a different level and are all the better for melting into the crowds as they walk out of Saint Anne's. It isn't an instant throw-away-your-crutches experience, but more devoted people connecting you with grace and loving kindness. I've even experienced groups of young doctors in training attend the service as part of their studies, giving them a different perspective on the body's ability to heal.

The second service I've been back to repeatedly, though not as often, is the twelve o'clock Mass at the Adoration Sisters on the Falls Road. I enjoy bringing others to it as a way of experiencing a short extract of connected Catholicism. The Adoration Sisters is the only service I've attended with Catholic nuns, The Poor Clare Monastery having closed in north Belfast, and there are so few of them around.

It's interesting to think that these are both weekday services that tend to have a devoted practicing congregation; portals of light in a city that so often seems to be in darkness.

Chapter 22: Religion as Cultural Identity

As the artist Professor Paul Seawright of Ulster University said to me once, "The problem is not with the people who go to church, but those who do not." Part of the issue with our historic difficulties in Northern Ireland is the issue of religion as cultural identity and people who historically identify as Protestant or Catholic but who don't have any belief system or attend to their own spiritual well-being. It's sometimes used as a hammer to verbally or physically beat someone up. It can be seen in proliferation around the twelfth of July when Orange parades are on. Many support it as an outpouring of Protestant culture but nothing to do with a spiritual tradition.

As I've mentioned before when I was based in Saint Martin's on the Newtownards Road for *Still Bunker*, the children of the area took an interesting in the activity within the church. Three young boys used to come every day and draw. One day they were telling us they belonged to East Belfast Protestant Boys marching band and demonstrated their marching and baton-twirling techniques. One day we told them we would do a tour for them around the different art pieces. We were in an area of the church where the font used to be and I asked them if they knew what it was. One boy explained that his cousin was christened and the others listened. I asked if any of them went to church. "My da says religion's boring," said one. None of them went to church regularly. I asked them if they knew that Protestantism was a spiritual practice. "No, it's not," one said. "It's this," and promptly walked around singing "The Sash|" miming beating a marching drum. This attitude is prevalent.

Many people on the nationalist side of the community will have come from a historically Catholic background and yet won't have any contemporary connection with the Catholic Church. The historical Protestant versus Catholic narrative is simplistic and binary in contemporary Belfast, not leaving room for the stories of alternative narratives and instead restates old traumas without giving room for new stories. The media tends to reify this.

At the launch of the 2018 4 Corners Festival I heard Reverend Norman Hamilton say in his opening remarks, "We need more people to show Christian virtues and less religion as cultural identity in Northern Ireland," but the difficulty lies in how to do this. Even the Northern Ireland Statistics Research Agency (NISRA) assumes the identity of individuals depending on where they live as opposed to what people actually say on their census forms. If you aren't seen as Catholic you must be Protestant. The equality monitoring forms for job applications were developed to try and ensure equality of opportunity in employment practices. They often ask about schooling, knowing that with our lack of integrated education and the majority of the population being educated along segregated lines, a person can be labelled easily.

In his MA Roy Fisher calls for a relook at the statistical data capture for the local population, declaring that a contemporary Northern Ireland society requires a contemporary lens to view its current population. But with the results of every census being used as a political football this needs to be done with great sensitivity.

Chapter 23: Protestants Have More Class

Given that I worked in the equality arena for a long time, at one point in my career I believed that most things could be sorted out by looking into equality legislation. It pained me to know and understand that which I couldn't quite figure out growing up. Culturally, those of us from the Protestant strands of religion in Northern Ireland have sometimes benefited from an unequal society. Protestants have more class, meaning that we've always had an upper, middle and working class, whereas Catholics were historically prejudiced against – denied basic rights and kept from certain professions so organize themselves differently. That's part of the reason why I pushed religion away growing up. How could it be of any use if it was responsible for such division?

The civil rights movement happened for a reason. At the fiftieth anniversary of the movement it can't be forgotten that working-class Protestants in some areas were living in squalor, but there was real prejudice against Catholics. The people I came across daily in all my years of cross-community work in Belfast are testament to it. Perhaps because of this something has stayed, developed and cultivated within people's spirits here that seems to be absent elsewhere.

I've heard it said that in Northern Ireland the divisions within the reformed traditions have added to the fractured sense of position and self of the Protestant community. Certainly there is a perception that working-class Protestants, as a divided group, have had more difficulty moving on. If you work your way up a social class you leave others behind – after all, how can you be middle or upper class if there's no one at the lower end of the scale? The Protestant middle and upper classes have little to gain by reaching out to the working classes, so they generally don't.

The reality I see in Northern Ireland is that many people have difficulty shifting out of warrior mode and into peacemaker mode. Native Americans had a process to help make this happen after times of war. Some people don't shift, or can't shift, because of viable threats; others don't because it seems their power and living is caught up with a warrior identity. If it goes, what do they have left? I've also heard it said that when the IRA was more active, many people were happy that loyalist paramilitaries were there, but once things moved on nobody wanted to help them shift out of out a warrior mindset. Republicans had Irish America to help them but loyalists lack outside help and are demonised for every shift they try to make.

The class issue was made clear to me at the Giro d'Italia in 2014. It seemed like the whole of Northern Ireland was in pink. There was an amateur art competition on the Newtownards Road but I didn't feel inclined towards it until the night before the race when I had a brainwave to make pink flower garlands and drape them around The Yardmen – a statue of three workmen coming from the shipyard, locally known as Westlife. I tweeted a picture of it to local politicians saying, "Aloha from East Belfast," and headed down to Portaferry to look after my dad. In the morning I looked at my social media to see that the statue's decoration had been added to – ribbons, hats, a cycle jersey and a pink plinth had all appeared. The press used it as a spot to record from and a tweet appeared of First Minister Arlene Foster, DUP, alongside Sammy Douglas, DUP MLA, staring at the statue, stating that they were delighted residents of Pitt Park were getting into the spirit of things. It made me smile. Sometimes I think that our visual language is so militarised that we need a little fun to break it up.

Back in east Belfast I walked up the Newtownards Road with Elvina Porter McCullough and the residents of Pitt Park invited me in for a burger. We talked about the flower garlands. "That was Mervyn across the road," they said. "No, it wasn't," we said, and explained how it had come about. A cordial hour was spent before we crossed the road to Westbourne Presbyterian. "What do you think of the statue?" we asked Mervyn Gibson. "That was the women across the road," he said. "No, it wasn't," I said, and explained what I'd done.

Around the church everyone had made a real effort of introducing pink anywhere they could – flowers, bicycles, bunting, scooters, signs, it was a carnival atmosphere. The garland incident seemed to me to be typical of the blame apportioning that goes on in Northern Ireland – it's always themuns over there – but there's evidence that hope and playfulness and art can be as effective for shifting a dynamic or narrative.

122

The streets were filled with local residents all the way up to Stormont. The generosity of the Newtownards Road residents disappeared when passing the more affluent of the Upper Newtownards Road where the barbecues were invite-only with crisp pink napkins and wine glasses set out in gardens for an exclusive Giro dining experience. By the time I reached Stormont I had to pay for everything myself and the class divisions within the cultural Protestant community were more obvious, each with their clearly defined social status. Status still exists and continues to be built on. The musical chairs of the class status natives are born into continues to colour their opportunities.

As I leave Joanmount Methodist Church in north Belfast I can see it's high up on the hill above a nationalist and republican part of the city in Ardoyne, an area which was heavily militarised during the Troubles and had one of the highest murder rates per square mile. There were great inequalities in the area and residents have experienced and sometimes inflicted immeasurable pain. Yet as I spoke with the congregation of Joanmount and walked out of the building, I could feel a spiritual flutter around me with the combined energy of the practicing congregation, some of whom have worshipped there for fifty years. Yes, there were inequalities, but how is it now in contemporary society? How has this affected our spirits and what positivity has it left behind now that the dust has settled twenty years on from the Good Friday Agreement?

I sit in Malone Presbyterian beside an elderly man who glows from the inside with a spiritual light. He has the look of a wealthy Protestant and probably comes from a long line of wealthy Protestants. I have republican friends who have nothing but contempt for him and anyone like him and they don't even know him, yet he glows with goodness and everyone around him shows him love and kindness. He is obviously cherished as an elderly member of the family. I ponder this during the shaking of hands to offer peace in the service as the tall man in front whom I offer my hand to skips me and reaches over my head to offer his hand to the man behind me first. I think of the words often written in front of many churches: "Visitors welcome". As I exit the church, I speak with the minister about what I'm doing. "Thank you for doing it," she said. "I will be able to say I shook your hand." Why is she thanking me?

2017 was the centenary of the Easter Rising and there were lots of commemorative events – but as with all events in Northern Ireland there wasn't one idea of how to do this. There had been a commemorative parade in the city but the People's Parade, organised by the Easter Rising Centenary Committee, wanted to do their own event differently. On the Sunday in question I drove into Belfast city centre thinking I would try and attend Berry Street Presbyterian for a service only to find that the city centre was surrounded by a ring of steel because of the parade. Looking for a plan B, I came across Saint Jude's and Christopher's, a church slightly outside the city centre that looked like a bunker. The church building was all that was left while all around the housing was demolished. I made my way over the threshold to be surprised by the brightness and love of care inside. Everywhere was gleaming with shiny brass, tapestry kneelers and fresh flowers. It seemed that there was to be a christening. A very proficient choir in full robes entered with the minister and the service started.

When the christening was about to take place, the godparents gathered around the font. At that moment the music coming from the republican march outside could be heard getting closer. The minister hesitated, waiting for the procession to pass, and as he christened the child into the Church of Ireland family, I couldn't help but think about the connection and disconnection between the two events: a christening in a Church of Ireland and the republican parade outside. Would this child have any future connection with the children involved in the parade outside? With the number of children who are educated separately in Northern Ireland, this child may not have an integrated education. What will he be told of the centenary in the future?

It was during 2017 that I realised I had been born in the fiftieth-anniversary year of the Easter Rising and this certainly had an effect on the population I was born into. We can be hopeful that at least the child wasn't born with the Troubles still raging, and be thankful to all those who made this possible, but as I write this section of the book we are yet again without a functioning assembly. Past hurts bubble up quickly to the surface on a weekly basis, and there is no sight of a resolution to the current status quo. We can only hope and work towards finding a chink of light to move towards.

Chapter 24: LGBTQ in the Church

Being born in 1966 and growing up in Northern Ireland, any school friends I had who were gay grew up surrounded by Christian traditions that had little room for them. Their questioning nature of their sexuality was shunned, ridiculed and despised. One friend was pointed at from the pulpit in a summer mission and denounced. Recently a report showed that sixty-eight per cent of children who are gay in the Northern Ireland school system have thought of suicide. This report wasn't acted upon when the assembly was up and running, which is in itself heartbreaking.

It was only in the nineties, when I went to the USA on a Fulbright Scholarship, that I saw for the first time a church in downtown New York with a sandwich board outside welcoming the LGBTQ community. It stopped me in my tracks. On a recent trip to Chicago I noticed a Presbyterian church with rainbow windsocks flying outside, making a sure statement of welcoming in the LGBTQ community. In my visits around the churches of Belfast I've found signs of a welcome for those from the LGBTQ community but none declaring from the outside like the church in central London that had on its noticeboard: Tuesday night is LGBTQ Christian night. However, during Belfast Pride 2018 All Souls Non-Subscribing Presbyterian in south Belfast had a Rainbow poster declaring an LGBTQ Communion service. In attending All Souls I have seen a glimpse of the amazing work they are doing with homeless people and also how a non – subscribing Presbyterian church can integrate and welcomes the LQBTQ community.

There are other signs of a thaw. In at the beginning of my church crawl I came to Saint George's a week after they had their annual International Day Against Homophobia and Biphobia (IDAHOT) service organised by Changing Attitude Ireland. It gave me so much hope to see that this was happening and it was almost permission to continue on my journey. In 2018 I attended their tenth annual church service for IDAHOT and listened while former bishop Trevor Williams spoke. His sermon was very humble. He spoke of his feeling that he needed to listen to the congregation instead of him preaching to them. He spoke of how God's love is for everyone, but that his gay friends had told him they didn't feel welcome. He spoke of a clergyman from the Iona Community who came to talk at their synod about a fourteen-year-old girl in his congregation who had died by suicide; of how they had found out that she had killed herself because she thought she was a lesbian and that God could never love her. This took them on a journey of making themselves an inclusive church and, as the founder of Corrymeela said, if churches they aren't in the business of reconciliation, they shouldn't be in the business at all. It seemed like the assembled congregation welcomed the opportunity to feel included alongside parishioners – welcomed back, in some instances, and welcomed for the first time in others. But there is still much work to be done.

Pádraig Ó Tauma during his time in Corrymeela has made great strides in leadership in this area. I've noticed an LBGTQ Christian retreat advertised for a number of years. For Belfast Pride's march 2016, now the biggest march in the city, I spotted the Methodist church in the actual parade. The Methodist Agápé Centre in south Belfast have opened a monthly evening group for LGBTQ with a particular interest in those who haven't felt welcome in any church before. This year at the Clonard Novena there was a whole homily on homophobia and only one person walked out. This is progress. In autumn there were further discussions in Clonard on this topic to see what the community need from the Catholic Church and what the Catholic Church needs from the community – after all, it's a two-way street. Karen Sethuraman of SoulSpace is also in leadership as part of the LGBTQ Christian Fellowship Spectrum in Belfast.

In England I see some discussion of transgendered bishops in the Anglican Communion. Many in the LQBTQ community in Northern Ireland believe that churches don't seek to include them anyway and therefore simply don't engage. If more church buildings were publicly declared for the LGBTQ community, I think it would welcome part of the population who don't feel included, and who certainly feel that there is a lack of understanding for their gifts. Yes, it would be seen as controversial by some but doesn't everyone have a soul and a spirit? There can be a smugness in some congregations that they alone own the truth, that the way they do church is the only way, and many people caught in the trauma of Northern Ireland depend on such beliefs.

Most recently the media reported that the Presbyterian Assembly voted to split from the Scottish Assembly due to their stance on christening children of same-sex relationships – the non-subscribing Presbyterian church having a more open interpretation of the gospel in this matter.

Sometimes people are told they can attend church but can't hold office – for instance the choir or positions of authority, or that they can join but not take Communion, which limits church involvement. There are, however, a number of same-sex married clergy in the Presbyterian church, both in the city and rural locations.

In getting feedback for this book, "The act itself is an abomination," was quoted to me a couple of times. If this is your view, many churches and congregations still hold it, but please don't use it to justify how churches treat the LGBTQ community or as a get-out clause to be inattentive to the divine. There are many waiting with open arms, ready to welcome LGBTQ people back into the fold, you just have to figure out where they are.

"I've heard of a school teacher who told children that they have a choice of being either male or female. To me this is child abuse," the minister went on to say it was in Scotland but as I looked around the church at the fifteen or so people who came out that Sunday, I felt that he was preaching about a very claustrophobic God. I could see that those congregants who followed his words were affected by it and it had developed their spirits in a restricted way, but I felt perhaps there needed to be less restriction. The minister who was preaching had been moved from a dying congregation and I could see why. The one he had moved from was now a vibrant multicultural, intergenerational church on the outskirts of Belfast. Soon he might be talking to himself.

I thought back to the recent article I'd read about the fluidity of gender and how when some Christian missionaries went on overseas missions, it was they who enforced male–female gender norms on the society they were working in. I thought about the Native Americans who came to Northern Ireland some time ago who had had a sex change to talk about how some of their tribes saw those with mixed gender as a gift, and how they have a special role to play in the workings of the tribe.

I thought about my visit to Gracehill, the male and female doors to enter the church and the male and female sections of the cemetery for people to be buried in. I thought about how well and good this is for people who fit within gender norms, but how much pain, suffering and desolation it can cause those who don't.

I think we're only at the beginning of welcoming the LGBTQ community into the church family. Harriet Long works for Women's Resource and Development Agency in Belfast. She works hard at creating space for conversations about the body, gender, sex, violence, trauma and recovery. As a theology graduate, she helped me understand that there is a whole body of academic research on viewing theological writing based on the gender norms of the time. Me thinks we're at the tip of an iceberg.

Chapter 25: No Sunday Service in the Village

Once in Portaferry, my husband and I went to Mass in Saint Patrick's Church. Walking up I spotted a group of men wearing black ties and thought there might be a funeral. My husband reassured me and said, "No, never on a Sunday," but as we entered it was obvious there was one – the support wheels were ready for a coffin.

As I sat waiting for the service to start, I thought about religion in the area. Someone in my family once told me that when my grandmother, "Ganger", as she was known, was getting married in the Church of Ireland a number of local Catholic women who she worked with came to the door to look in as they were forbidden to enter. The minister then came down and shut the door so they couldn't see the wedding service. Sitting among the contemporary congregation of Saint Patrick's, built in 1762, with the congregants glowing from the inside, I thought about this division. The choir, all female, was really beautiful singing in joyful harmony. The church was full and had the simple familiarity that a village congregation has, shaking hands and smiling at one another. The priest spoke about how unusual it was to have a funeral on a Sunday but as there were two the following day and a big one later in the week, it was a necessity. I listened to his words, amazed at the difference I felt from when I first started going to church. The physical sensation of light entering my body from the inside out, lighting up from the inside; a space inside my head hummed with its own energy and liquid light seemed to flow. The feeling persisted for much of the day and as I write this now, I can feel it again.

One of my sister's neighbours sat beside us, and I explained that we hadn't realised there was a funeral. When it came to having Communion, the priest explained that if we only wanted a blessing, we should come up and cross our hands so he would know. Once Mass was over, we took a walk in the graveyard. The coffin was being placed in the ground – fields of sheep to one side, Strangford Lough to the other. A beautiful place to rest your bones. The altar boys and girls in their gowns took their incense and weaved their way back through the gravestones. The family of the deceased ninety-one-year-old man filtered through the tombstones. My husband noted that he recognised many names on the gravestones now: Beck, McAlea, McNamara, Dummigan. After seventeen years in Northern Ireland he was becoming a local. In the Church of Ireland graveyard in the village what I notice is that a whole generation of people I remember when I was growing up are now buried there. The graveyard is filling up and the church is not. How will this evolve in another fifty years? Who knows?

On other occasions I've attended services in the Methodist and Ballyphilip Church of Ireland, where I was christened and confirmed. The Presbyterian church has been turned into a cultural centre called Portico but still has a congregation meeting every Sunday. I'm minded when I visit the village and want discretion to see if I want to start attending a church, the whole village knows and it's hard to be discreet. Sometimes I suggest people visit a Belfast church instead. It makes it easier to be anonymous and explore different options without the village watching on.

There are no church services on the other side of the lough in Strangford on a Sunday any more. Saint Mary Star of the Sea in Strangford has a vigil Mass on Saturday night. In Christ Church, Ballyculter, a service my older sister and I sometimes walked the three miles to as children rotates among the Lecale Area Mission Partnership (LAMP) churches for services. An article in the *Down Recorder* on 11 June 2014 highlighted the lack of Catholic priests:

> *"Statistics compiled by the church in the first stage of this review were published this week and show there are now only thirteen priests across the Downpatrick area ... and twelve across the Newcastle area."*

The grade B1 Presbyterian church in Strangford was built in 1845 and has been derelict since 2003. It has recently been sold and luckily refurbished. The chapel on the de Ros estate has infrequent services, many weddings and a lovely Christmas morning service where people are encouraged to bring along an instrument if the play one. This decline happened very quickly over a period of thirty-five years when previous to that everyone in the village would have attended a service.

Not to have a Sunday service of any kind in a village would have been unthinkable in the past but is simply a numbers game now.

In the south of France, where my mother-in-law lives, the priest of the Catholic church is only in attendance one in every four Sundays. The rest of the time lay people, both men and women from the village, take the services, including funerals, something we haven't yet seen in Ireland. Would it be accepted? Would anyone have any say in the matter?

The Methodist and Church of Ireland have an agreement to share clergy in some instances. Some housing estates, for example, have Methodist, Presbyterian and Church of Ireland churches as well as perhaps a gospel hall, and all for a small estate it seems madness, but then a precedent for religious freedom has been a long and hard battle to win. On Pope Francis' visit to Ireland in 2018 there was much discussion about the great opportunity for the laity within the church to take on more roles as the decline in vocations continues. On the one hand I think that church has become less of an essential in many people's lives, but on the other hand people who are struggling or are burdened and finding life's path difficult have forgotten that challenging circumstances are exactly what the church is supposed to help with – give up your burdens. Certainly the pit of anger I used to have in my stomach has simply disappeared. I'm constantly coming across people who are struggling with all matters of daily occurrences, terminal illness being just one, yet they haven't remembered or heard that God can alleviate their suffering or walk alongside them in their grief as they are unable to get past the tabloid media perception of religion. Some churches lack the mechanisms to offer pathways into their congregations. For example, there are still some churches I haven't visited because I simply can't work out the time of services because their websites and signage haven't been updated.

Chapter 26: So, Which Church is Right?

A few years into my church visits I was pondering a question: if there is such a thing as God, then who is right about it? Difficult past experiences with me seem to have been swept away. As the women of the Church of God, Shankill Road, said to me, "In Northern Ireland we have so much baggage about religion." If it leaves you with the definite feeling that humans have spirits and there is such a thing as God, what do you do? Who do you follow to deal with it? Do you need to follow something? Is it the Bible and if so, which translation? What of the Koran, Bhagavad Gita, the Sutras? Some churches are under attack from stories of abuse and wrongdoing, others from a world view of exclusion and fundamentalism. Some people ask me what church I'll attend once I've gone around them all. Others say you don't have to be a churchgoer to be a good person. Yes, that's true, but there's another dimension that I slipped into simply by attending services whatever the denomination or teachings; an internal lightness and luminosity is physically palpable with me at all times.

Brian Ervine, former leader of the Progressive Unionist Party, PUP, said to me, "Christians have more in common. All churches are agreed on the apostles and Nicene Creed, and the rise of secularism is the common enemy of them all," so maybe it doesn't matter as long as it's something that people follow.

What of Buddhists? Buddha consciousness – or Christ consciousness – is a belief that everyone can reach. Each stream of Buddhism shows how this can be achieved in different ways. There are many paths to follow – some leading one way, some leading another. If you look on the floor of Saint Anne's Cathedral, there is a labyrinth. You can follow the dark side or the light side; each leads to a different place.

If God exists, what we have in Northern Ireland is perhaps many different ways to deal with it or different ways to uncover God. Churches have evolved over time – sometimes through disagreements, reforms, fallouts, divine inspiration, inspired leaders who can see different ways of doing things, political manoeuvrings, fear or land grabs. I even found one that was formed because it did not believe in renting pews. Throw that in with patriarchy and you have a fine soup of positions. If this is the case, then they all have their truths. Each one, if practised earnestly over a period of time, would develop a spirit in a particular way and offer resilience in another way. The danger perhaps comes when people believe that their way is the only way and subsequently separate themselves from any fellowship with other denominations. If you are a church that has existed for fifty years and you say you are the only one, what happened to God before then? What are these man-made rules – and which man made them? So much of it comes down to personal choice: do you like to sing, what tradition were you brought up in, does any of it still appeal to you, do you like wearing hats? Some people I've met can't bear to think of themselves developing their spirituality along the same lines as their parents; others can't stand any hypocrisy they see in the church they were brought up in but because of the legacy of the Troubles can't contemplate investigating a religion that they see as "the other". Yet still, week after week, many in the population attend services and continue to practice in their chosen religious denomination, but it still doesn't answer the question of who is right.

Well, maybe they all are. What if all spiritual traditions believe that humans have a spiritual dimension and that over a series of practices and faith humans can develop that side of themselves, keeping on a path. The complexity of the matter regarding Northern Ireland is that some denominations have a history of persecution, of elitism, inequality, status, power and control, yet contemporary congregations have love and forgiveness at their core. Looking into the eyes of an elderly Methodist man who has practised his religion all his life, you can see his lightness of spirit, the glow and twinkle of goodness. To some in our community he is everything that they hate: a white male perceived privileged Protestant. I've met many people who've been so wounded by hurts of the past that they can't look beyond these labels; hardened by hate or traumatic experiences.

All hail the leaders who are trying to transform this perspective. I remember going to a reconciliation conference once – one of many things that our peace process has turned into a business. They said that it takes three generations to properly look at reconciliation; the distance needed to view events in a different manner. Attitudes soften with time but not enough to make sweeping changes across the board. There have been many in church families who have worked towards unity and ecumenical sharing before and through the Troubles: unity without uniformity. There is also the contemporary Christianity grouping of mostly Protestants stating that there are spiritual lessons to be learned from the Troubles. Beyond the more obvious ones this is a perspective that many might find difficult for obvious reasons.

Christianity in cultural contention, the term highlights the condition that some in Northern Ireland find themselves whether with a faith or not. The contention of our collective past means that this is the lens through which we live our lives, requiring time and distance before seeing it any other way. Often with much resistance. I think what we've developed in Northern Ireland is a kind of living history of religions and all in such a small area of the world. We have so many different varieties of Christianity in particular. Some of the more evangelical churches say that they aren't Catholic or Protestant, labelling themselves simply as Christian, trying to disassociate themselves from traditional animosities. I suspect that it matters less what a person's denomination is other than the fact that they have one.

So, coming back to the question of who's right. Maybe what we should all be pointing out is that within Northern Ireland we have a large community of people who, although divided into numerous denominations, believe that humanity has a spiritual aspect to it, and that maybe in today's increasingly secular consumer-driven world this is the important common denominator – that actually there is more that unites than divides. Does saying who is right come down more to an aspect of personal choice about the style of service or the type of communal experience each person prefers?

If you want to bring it down to a debate on theology, I couldn't answer with any authority. There are many others who have much more learning and understanding than me. All I know is that starting from a position of not believing in God, just being a bit annoyed when God was mentioned, but experiencing unusual energetic happenings in my secular life, I've come on an odyssey that has completely transformed my inner life and seems to have cleansed me of everything that has gone before. I've been deeply challenged. I remember it was a couple of years in, against my logical reasoning, that I started to believe that God existed as I felt the difference church attendance had made to my life. The mystery of faith. Now I can't imagine this not being part of my life, as is the case with other people who practice their spiritual tradition and gain much from it.

Chapter 27: Conclusions

Walking down Royal Avenue in Belfast city centre I see a man in his sixties singing a hymn and giving out a tract. I cross the road to pick one up and he smiles and nods at me. Fifty metres on a small group of people stand with a microphone giving testament to their living faith. I collect a leaflet from them too. The young man takes his turn at the microphone to tell the shoppers how his life was full of sin and then he accepted the Lord and his life changed so much for the better. People ignore him, but I smile and listen.

On I walk past the afternoon drinking crowd outside Kelly's Cellars, noticing how different the shape of their energy bodies is to those in many of the churches and chapels I've visited. They're out for a pint, a bit of craic, perhaps caught in a never-ending cycle, perhaps not. On I go to Saint Mary's, thick with a spiritual resonance. I sit down and watch as people come and light candles and say a prayer. The Holy Spirit moves around the city, calling us forth. People are distracted with their worries, intergenerational trauma is rife – you can see it in the faces of the locals, watch them and compare their faces to the faces of the tourists. The tourists who don't carry the burden of our history and sufferings, yet want a one-hour tour to understand what we ourselves still can't quite comprehend after six hundred years. Some people stop and connect with the whisper, others, as I've heard Reverend Steve Stockman say, feel so far away from God that they eventually disconnect from themselves. Yet there is always a way back.

Could it be that if not the meaning then surely the outcome of all this traumatic activity in Northern Ireland, the north of Ireland, is that it is an ancient storehouse for different spiritual streams of energy? Has this been captured at a time when the world needs it most? Could there be a similar impact of Columbanus over one thousand four hundred years ago – a need for this energy to stream out over other lands? There is such a great need for healing to be done, and the world needs hope.

I've purposely not wanted to reduce this exploration of church attendance simply to statistics. In fact, on a number of occasions I've set out to write a statistical chapter and found that I couldn't. I'm aware that although I didn't set out to focus on Christian traditions in the city, around ninety per cent of my visits have been to congregations of Christian denomination. There are many vibrant faiths within the city, and it is my intention to visit all of them because to simply visit one of each denomination is useful but superficial; bringing awareness but not the deep spiritual shift of my experience.

With changing church attendance patterns, some churches are under threat of closure. At a rough guess, taking into consideration empty seats, if half the churches closed, there would be room for their congregations in the other half. But this, in many instances, would destroy the diversity on offer – perhaps some spiritual strands would disappear altogether? We are nothing if not radically independent in Belfast. In Belfast church attendance is higher than in many regions of the UK and Ireland. Christianity in particular gets a bashing in the media, but unless there's a radical shift church closures will speed up within the next twenty years and that means that some of these portals of light may disappear.

The population shifts happening in the city shift the spiritual landscape of a place. For instance, Saint Brigid's Catholic Church in Malone, south Belfast, has seen an increase in congregation for major religious holidays as west Belfast, which has traditionally been Catholic, moves further south, which is more mixed. The reformed churches in the area have depleting congregations. Vocations are also an issue. Churches that have opened their arms to female clergy have managed to deal with this decline in vocations with wonderful new energy and enthusiasm, but there are still not enough. On the Pope's visit to Ireland in 2018 there was talk of the new-found opportunities for laypeople that have come about with the lack of vocations for priests, so who knows what will happen. Some denominations do not allow part-time posts, limiting the skills and opportunities for those with caring responsibilities further. There is also an issue with some clergy not being equipped to connect with people where they are or new congregants coming to a service or a fete not really feeling welcomed or simply acknowledged. This I've observed or experienced on numerous occasions when congregations are busy talking with each other instead of welcoming anyone new. In the past I've been given books, invited to courses, given religious tracts, asked if I was born-again, saved, and these just made me build barriers. In fact, these barriers were built in my teenage years when a daily prospect of being blown to bits was played out on our streets and TV screens as well as in our daily lives all in the name of religion, so to me it felt justified, as no doubt it was and still is for others as well. An invisible wall was just as real as the physical walls that divide many people in Belfast. All I thought at the time was to hunker down, focus on art and get out. Saving some of my dinner money to spend on a bottle of cider also helped – hey, we had to entertain ourselves somehow!

I've often wondered why this has happened to me. Not feeling worthy most of the time, I have to be reminded that the development of the spirit is available to everyone no matter who they are or what they've done in the past. I am sure there are many people out there who have met me at a different stage of this journey, who cannot understand the person I am today but connection with the divine is open to all – yes, that means you as well.

Some clerics haven't had the gift of not believing in God at some point in their lives. The clergy by and large have a lot of biblical knowledge, the love of Christ has developed for them a bottomless source of teachings and learning, far more than me, but people have to be open to receive it in the right conditions. What is the point of all that training if no effort is made in connecting with people outside their original congregations or taking the time to figure out just how to do it? Some congregations have no real understanding of what is happening in other churches in other parts of the city. Some share pulpits around Easter but the long-term connections like those of Clonard Monastery and Fitzroy Presbyterian Church are exceptions. Parish boundaries and diocese boundaries of different congregations divide the administration of the Holy Spirit – sometimes to such an extent that the general public can't see the wood for the trees. They are confused. I also feel that some of the clergy feel trapped within a system. Many people only see the church as a point of trauma, sound bites played out in the media, and can't see the love behind it.

You either believe that humans have a spirit or not. If yes, then what do you do to deal with it? At its core is simply love. God exists, and what you do in your life has an impact on how the soul develops and what is revealed to you. I never realised that churchgoing could have such a physical effect on a person going to services. Belfast has turned into an open-air living museum to the life of the spirit. I can see with my own eyes how faith or spiritual practice shapes the soul of different individuals. You can see how generations of people drawn into the city have stayed within their genetic group, by this I mean many congregations share their ancestors' physical characteristics. If you take the time with open-hearted generosity to explore the city with this in mind, you'd be amazed at the quality of the soul or spirit energy that people within its loose boundaries have.

As you take this journey and follow the whispering of your soul, you might be heartened on a cold winter morning by the welcome and warmth you receive. You'll hear singing developed in another age, services that are more like raps, but you'll also notice class divisions, wonder why so few Catholic men in some areas attend church, be amazed at the churches that are like nightclubs or musicals. Many cups of tea and coffee will be offered as well as a donut or two, either before or after the service. An uplifting will happen as perhaps you sit and rage against any of it being true, or if you're a believer, you might chuckle at God's alternative plan for the city. But if you stick at it, a shift might occur internally until one day you'll experience joy for the simple reason of being alive.

You'll have doubts but the winter months will no longer draw in on you as you carry a lightness of spirit everywhere you go. Life's challenges that come to you will become easier to deal with. You might feel like a fish out of water sometimes, unsure of when to sit or stand, but you'll feel a spiritual strength walk alongside you when dealing with people who are suffering or dying, even when you don't request it. In inner light might appear. If you're lucky and keep following the journey, you'll wonder how all these different strands of spirituality came about. You'll experience listening to someone speaking, singing or preaching in tongues, feel an inner calm, rid yourself of all misunderstanding while the knots in your soul dissolve.

Christmas will return to being magical. People will notice the difference in you. It won't all happen overnight, and the ironic thing is that I don't think you need to believe when you start, but it will creep up on you as time goes on. Some people will try and put you off – in fact, you may try and put yourself off. You'll need to ignore people who say you could never be one of them until you find yourself in a parallel universe. If you combine this with an editing of your media consumption and look at art more often, the effect will amplify quicker. But it might all depend on the weight of your soul to begin with, and change takes time.

There is an assortment of people who are practising spiritually in the city. Over a concentrated period of time, this has an effect on the individuals concerned. These faith practices have developed and evolved to offer humans an extraordinarily large array of different religious freedoms. In the Western world we can currently experience a great selection of religious practices that historically hasn't always been the case. In gathering feedback for this book one person told me the word I should use is "faith" not "practice"; however, when I started this exploration, I didn't have a faith, but the practice of church attendance connected me to another world entirely.

At the end of many Belfast streets there's a building in which people can explore these traditions. Quite often within the Protestant reformed traditions there are two or three different options to choose from within a short walking distance. Of personal significance to me is that I openly admit that if I had had children, I wouldn't have had them christened, such was my attitude towards the church. I didn't want to instil any conditioning towards any divisions in any sons or daughters. Now I can see the confusion for some parents in deciding their children's spiritual needs – if they think they have any, and the confusion of some children as a result. Is that partly the reason for our suicide epidemic? Or the reticence towards encouraging children to practice their spirituality with no belief in anything else other than what we see, pressure on how we look, what we wear, how we consume. The peer and societal pressure to go to church that existed when I grew up is no longer there.

Life can be hard, growing up in contemporary society can be difficult, but why are there so many young people who would rather die than be with us in our contemporary reality? The Troubles have left behind much in terms of trauma, large pieces of some people's lives were heavily disrupted, if they managed to survive at all. This gets passed on through generations. The alternative narratives of victim and perpetrator are played out in our media daily, and they also live among us. The media reify the trauma stories, allowing the same voices to be heard, all but ignoring an alternative viewpoint. For some parents wearily opting out has been their decision. The Church of Ireland talks of a lost generation.

Now that I've a changed mind, I would christen my children if I had any (unless I decided to be a Baptist) and encourage spiritual exploration. I often notice the difference between the parents and children I see attending church and, if I visit St George's Market afterwards, those who are not. The churchgoing children and parents seem to have a wider circle of support in the congregations, their children are bright and cheerful, feeling loved, given an explanation of life. While in St George's Market the non-churchgoing families may be well fed and dressed but they often look tired and distracted, lacking in cohesion and support for life's difficult task of parenting. They are without wider support or that extra twinkle; often with a blankness in their gaze. All churches have child protection policies these days with some developing minibus collection routes for kids who attend without their parents.

Children are being sexualised younger, confused about life, choices and moral behaviours, perhaps looking to video games and pornography to fill any educational gaps their parents aren't filling in. I heard a minister once talk of *Lady Chatterley's Lover* as the thing to get your hands on as a boy. Now you just switch on TV to see sexualised behaviour. The reality is, however, young people are accessing it on their phones. The parental pressure, vigilance and requests to go to church in whole areas has ebbed way. Should making money and consumerism be the focus of people lives?

People are in great need of updating their sectarianism as many are holding onto images and observations that came from their grandparents one hundred years ago and are no longer relevant in the twenty-first century. Attitudes formed in another age with real fears and concerns in mind are passed on as an intergenerational mantel. It's time to let some things go. Will you join me in doing so?

I am content. I wonder if the plan for Northern Ireland was to hold all these different strands of religion close by in one place; a kind of living history for the spirit where seekers could move from church to church and receive an opening of their souls, a softening of their hearts. Maybe this is the lotus in the mud, the famous Buddhist value: "Like a lotus flower that grows out of the mud and blossoms above the muddy water surface, we can rise above our defilements and sufferings of life." After all, Belfast has had plenty of suffering. We have held onto something here that has slipped away almost unnoticed in other parts of the world. What if it slipped away from the world entirely?

Much of this journey was taken in an unconscious manner. When people asked me what I was doing I couldn't explain and just said, "I'm in transition." From what and to what I couldn't explain; just following a thread as artists do, unsure where it might lead but knowing that the desire to follow the thread held importance for me beyond which I was able to verbally articulate. I, like many others, had a feeling that something was out of balance. The physical collapse I'd experienced at work was my body's way of telling me that something had to change, even though my head tried to deny it. I was heartened to find out that those who experience trauma can develop amazing resilience. I had a strong sense of needing to stay in Northern Ireland, which is sometimes hard for others to understand what with my education and experience – to say nothing of a French husband who speaks five languages. "Why are you here?" people would ask. "I feel there is something I need to do here," was sometimes my reply. Perhaps now I've found it.

This church attendance has led me on an adventure that has completely changed my perceptions and the direction of my life. It was as if something was whispering me on. I could have, at any time, chosen to ignore it or filled my life with so much activity and technological distraction that I couldn't see or hear the whisper. At times I tried to but I'm glad I didn't and now know that I've further to travel. Is this a journey you might be on too?

I started out with an open-minded curiosity in a secular media-dominated world with inordinate real and perceived barriers of looking at religion in Northern Ireland combined with a background of coalface community economic development which made me ill, stuck as I was in the traumatic, combative, bitching, backbiting structure that holds the city and the trauma within together. Peace funds brought opportunities but as there was so much money involved

143

it created a structure of consultants and organisations who thought that the word "peace" had moved from meaning the absence of conflict to meaning money. It was time for something else.

I heard Professor Brandon Hamber, director of Incore at Ulster University, say at a Nichiren Buddhism Peace Conference that it made him aware that many people believe that peace can be delivered as a paperwork exercise with administration, yet Buddhism, for example, and I would add in Christianity, has an ancient person-centred wisdom practice to bring about peace. A focus on inner peace which ripples out into everything you do.

I'm sitting in my house on a cold January morning, no longer noticing the darkness as it doesn't exist. It no longer pushes into me, or is pushed further into my being by the daily media diet of doom and gloom beamed into my living room keeping me in fear, keeping my consciousness at a lower level, stuck on buying products, how to have beautiful hair, smooth skin, nice clothes, great eyebrows, the next holiday bringing about relief, looking for status in my work life or moving me towards the potential tombstone epitaph of: "I consumed, I watched TV".

I was stuck in a world of striving and competition, not remembering that anything else existed; one of the busy, harassed women you see around town, busy around shops, busy driving around, busy in offices, snappy, determined, focused, harassed, like the one I noticed in the supermarket saying that the distressed elderly woman couldn't go first in the queue as she herself had spent so much time finding a parking space and she was just so busy. She had no time to be kind and thoughtful, no time to consider how that woman came to be distressed, that she was showing the first signs of dementia. Perhaps she thought she could buy a face cream for that as well? She ran out the door as she purchased her lifestyle magazine on how to have it all, trapped in a never-ending cycle of work-to-consume. Oh, but there's always that glass or five of wine to keep you going.

Now it's as if a parallel universe has opened up; one where life flows from one minute to the next. The beauty of the present moment dominates and all around the change to my inner life is extraordinary. This challenge will never be over. I'm certain that I've started a lifelong love of church services and a desire to share with others what I've found. I'm curious to see if anyone would repeat my experience and see if they get the same results. The question is: would they have to be a printmaker first? What is the alchemy that happens to a person in the mandala of the taught printmaking process? As we look at the complexity of religion in the city, we very often look at the negatives that religion has brought: abuse, inequalities, murder and mayhem, a militarised population, traumatised media, traumatised political class, some who are trying to heal personally at the same time as leading, some keeping divisions going so that they can stay in charge. After finding a spot in the trauma in which to make their living, some don't want to let it go. The warrior spirit is alive and well in the city and it doesn't easily transform itself or soothe into submission. In Belfast "Protestant" and "Catholic" are synonymous with division, but if you turn that around to ask who is suffering, you look at it through a different lens. Still many in the population of Belfast hold religion and churchgoing as a central tenant to their daily and weekly lives; the fellowship a core tenet of being.

Here in this northern tip of Europe a spiritual sensibility has been held onto. There are no longer swings being chained up in the play parks on a Sunday – in fact the city boasts a whole network of refurbished play parks. With the daily battering of Christianity in the media, it's easy to assume that anti-gay rights, fundamentalism and abuse dominate the church story. It's important not to brush these aspects under the carpet but it's also important to note that love and forgiveness, two of the central tenants of most religions, are in dire need of manifesting in the wider population. Goodness works. Love is more than just an emoji. You can see it in the street pastors, the food banks, the faith-based homeless hostels and care homes, the churches focused on helping young people out of addiction. You can see it in the Cinnamon Network supporting faith-based social enterprise, in Root Soup at the L'Arche community, in Loveworks, and in businesses that have the central practices of faith at their core, sprung out of the Presbyterian church.

The congregations of Belfast are holding onto a light and a knowledge that have disappeared in other places. We have a large percentage of the population who have been worshipping together in the same place, sometimes for generations. This has created an energy that is easy to tap into and available at the end of most streets. Perhaps this is the reason for it all? Perhaps we are holding onto this for others? Perhaps it's because of the quality of the soul of this place that all this happened? Or maybe it's simply a happy result of a horrific history. Whatever the answer, we're here now and it no longer matters so much about your religious affiliation in terms of jobs, housing or opportunities – although some state otherwise. We are free to choose and so many choose the secular, but still in Belfast people of all ages continue to strive for love and goodness and knowing God instead of seeing the divisions within the different denominations. Perhaps it's time to see the common thread within a large body of people who continue to believe in a higher power and human spirituality, even if they're hidden from each other behind walls of stone and stained glass and in some cases military-grade barriers.

In my own journey my mind is firmly made up that humans do indeed have a spirit. God exists. The things you do in life affect your soul and whether it can dull and harden or brighten and soften. The beauty of Christianity in particular allows for constant forgiveness and constant renewal. Without these pockets of light in the city of Belfast, darkness might have swallowed us up years ago. I'm completing my churchgoing odyssey as a different person, a better person from the one I was before. It has physically changed my inner landscape for the better, brought a sense of peace and calm never before experienced, rekindled a love of singing, shifted an egocentricity that was firmly established by an art college education, washed away any darkness that lurked in my godless life and brought unimagined blessings. I hope that you feel this too, or if not, that you perhaps take time to explore if it's possible in this wonderful and wounded city of ours. God bless you.

Biography

Born in Newtownards in 1966 to Frances and Paddy Lawson, who had returned to Northern Ireland to oversee the design and building of the Ulster Museum extension, Bronagh spent her first two years on the Upper Newtownards Road with her three older sisters before moving to Portaferry in 1968. After Frances and Paddy separated in the seventies, the girls and Frances moved to a council house in Strangford. Educated at Down High School, Downpatrick, in 1986 Bronagh attended art college in Bristol and then gained a first-class degree in textiles fashion at Winchester School of Art, Hampshire. Moving to London on graduation, she won a Fulbright Scholarship and attended Parsons School of Design in New York. Bronagh sometimes visited Northern Ireland and despaired. Returning to Northern Ireland from New York pre-ceasefire, she spent time as a participant on various cross-community development programmes before deciding to use her creativity in a different way. For thirteen years she set up and ran cross-border cross-community development programmes mostly within the enterprise sector in interface areas of Belfast. Within this gift of a time she investigated her own socialisation of being brought up in rural coastal Northern Ireland during the Troubles, and heard many stories from people in the city similar to life she saw only on the TV growing up – and often switched off as it was so horrific. She spent three years based in north Belfast, between republican New Lodge and loyalist Tiger's Bay. Walking into work one day she collapsed. She had become incapable of processing the trauma that people living in some of the most-deprived wards of Europe at the time brought in with them daily. Disillusioned with the traumatised structures that had developed around the peace-dividend, wounded, she found herself coming back to her original training as an artist and hence started a journey towards her own healing. This book is a true account of that time and it's unusual unfolding outcome.

Appendix: List of Churches Visited

The list below shows all my visits to churches, with date and time (AM unless otherwise stated) of service.

12/2008	Unsure	Dublin
Unsure	11:00	Knock Methodist Church, Belfast
Unsure	11.30	Knock Presbyterian Church, Belfast
19/04/2009	11:00	Gilnahirk Presbyterian Church, Belfast
03/05/2009	10.45	Tullycarnet Presbyterian Church, Belfast
10/05/2009	10.30	Saint Molua's Church, Belfast
17/05/2009	10.30	Saint Mark's Church, Dundela
24/05/2009	11:00	Kirkpatrick Memorial Presbyterian Church, Belfast
01/06/2009	10:00.	Ballyphilip and Ardquinn, Portaferry
07/06/2009	10:00	Saint George's Church, Belfast
16/08/2009	11:00	Killyleagh Parish Church, Killyleagh (baptism)
23/09/2009	11:00	Saint Colmcille, Donegal
30/09/2009	11:00	Westbourne Presbyterian Church, Belfast
04/10/2009	10:00	Saint Matthew's, Belfast
11/10/2009	11:00	May Street Presbyterian, Belfast (now Central Church)
11/11/2009	10:15	Saint Dorothea's Church, Gilnahirk
29/11/2009	10:45	Saint Mark's Church, Dundela
06/12/2009	11:00	Mountpottinger Methodist Church, Belfast
13/12/2009	10:30	Saint Columba's Parish Church, Knock
20/12/2009	7:00 PM	Holy Trinity Glencraig, Holywood (carols by candlelight)
25/12/2009	10:00	Paroisse Saint-Francois D'Assise en Nyonsais, Nyons, France
03/01/2010	11:00	Bethel Baptist, Knock Dual Carriageway (Castlereagh Fellowship)
10/01/2010	11:30	Sandown Free Presbyterian Church, Belfast
19/01/2010	10:00	Newtownards Road Elim Church, Belfast
26/01/2010	11:30	Albert Bridge Congregational Church, Belfast
31/01/2010	11:00	Saint Patrick's Church of Ireland, Ballymacarrett
01/03/2010	11:00	Bloomfield Baptist Church (now Village Church Belfast)
08/03/2010	11:30	Calvary Baptist Church, Belfast
21/03/2010	PM	Sweat Lodge, Wicklow Mountains
04/04/2010	11:00	Holy Trinity Glencraig, Holywood (christening)
11/04/2010	11:00	Down Cathedral, Downpatrick
18/04/2010	10:30	Saint Martin's Church Ballymacarrett (now Saint Martin's Centre)
25/04/2010	3:00 PM	Caroline Gallagher, Portrush (healer)
02/05/2010	11:30	Holy Cross Dunfanaghy Catholic Church, Donegal
09/05/2010	11:30	Mountpottinger Presbyterian Church, Belfast
16/05/2010	11:00	Bloomfield Presbyterian Church, Belfast
23/05/2010	11:00	Saint Anne's Cathedral, Belfast
01/06/2010	10:00	Saint George's, Belfast (matins)
06/06/2010	10:00	Chapeltown Chapel (near Strangford)
12/06/2010	1:00 PM	Blessing RNLI lifeboat dedication, Portaferry
13/06/2010	10:00	Templemore Hall Assembly, Templemore Avenue, Belfast
27/06/2010	11:00	McQuiston Memorial Presbyterian Church, Belfast

04/07/2010	11:30	Iron Hall, Templemore Avenue, Belfast
18/07/2010	10:00	Saint George's Parish Church, Belfast
24/07/2010	11:00	Down Cathedral, Downpatrick
01/08/2010	11:00	Baptist Assembly, Albertbridge Road (now Kingdom Harvest Church)
08/08/2010	11:00	Cregagh Presbyterian, Belfast
22/08/2010	10:00	Saint Patrick's Church of Ireland, Ballymacarrett
05/09/2010	10.30	Newtownbreda Presbyterian Church, Belfast
12/09/2010	10:30	Holy Rosary Parish, Belfast
26/09/2010	09:30	Saint Malachy's Church, Belfast
09/10/2010	11:30	Saint Finnian's Church, Belfast
16/10/2010	11:30	Saint Michael in-the-hamlet, Liverpool
23/10/2010	11:30	Mountpottinger Baptist Church, Belfast
31/10/2010	10:00	Willowfield Parish Church, Belfast
31/10/2010	11:30	Martyrs' Memorial Free Presbyterian Church, Belfast
11/2010	1:30 PM	Dockers' Club, Sailortown, Belfast (SHIP remembrance service)
25/12/2010	11:00	Église Réformée, Nyons, France (Reformed Church)
31/01/2011	11:30	Saint Clement's, Templemore Avenue, Belfast
31/01/2011	08:30	Saint George's Parish Church, Belfast
20/02/2011	11:00	Belfast Central Mission, Belfast
27/02/2011	10:00	Saint Paul's and Saint Barnaba's, Belfast
13/03/2011	10:15	Journey Towards Healing Conference, BBC morning service, Europa Hotel, Belfast
20/03/2011	10:30	Belmont Presbyterian Church, Belfast
27/03/2011	09:30	Clonard Monastery, Belfast (pre-restoration)
03/04/2011	10.30	Saint Elizabeth's Church, Dundonald
17/04/2011	11:00	Parkgate Avenue Gospel Hall, Belfast
24/04/2011	10:00	Portaferry Methodist Church, Portaferry
01/05/2011	11:00	Sydenham Methodist Church, Belfast
10/05/2011	2 days	Miranda Macpherson Retreat
01/05/2011	10:45	Saint Mark's Church, Dundela
29/05/2011	12:00PM	Saint Patrick's Church, Donegall Street, Belfast
08/06/2011	11:30	Liverpool Cathedral, Liverpool (confirmation)
12/06/2011	10:30	Saint Paul and Saint Barnabas, Belfast
15/06/2011	11:00	Light of the world (unsuccessful church plant)
19/06/2011	09:00	Christian Fellowship Church (CFC), Belmont
23/06/2011	11:00	Clonard Monastery, Belfast, Novena (temporary tent during refurbishments
26/06/2011	11:00	Saint Paul's, Belfast
07/08/2011	10:00	Holy Cross Passionists, Belfast
14/08/2011	Unsure	Sandown Road Free Presbyterian
28/08/2011	10:00	Christian Fellowship Church (CFC), Belmont
11/09/2001	Unsure	Branagh Memorial Church, Belfast
18/09/2011	11:00	Connsbrook Avenue Congregational Church, Belfast
25/09/2011	11:30	Saint Donard's Church of Ireland, Belfast
06/11/2011	11:15	New Life City Church, Northumberland Street, Belfast
08/12/2011	PM	Merci Marie, Lyon (festival of light)
19/11/2011	Half day	Women in Faith Conference, Cavehill Methodist Church, Belfast
11/12/2011	Unsure	Cathédrale Notre-Dame de Paris, Paris, France
24/12/2011	9:00 PM	Saint Peter's Cathedral, Belfast (Christmas Eve Mass)
10/01/2012	11:00	Saint Patrick's, Portaferry (funeral)
15/01/2012	11:30	Saint John's, Orangefield, Belfast
22/01/2012	10:00	Exchange Church, Belfast

29/01/2012	11:30	Saint Andrew's Presbyterian Church, Belfast
04/02/2012	11:00	Rehoboth Evangelical Mission, Mount Vernon, Belfast
11/02/2012	10:00	Haven Hall, York Road Baptist Fellowship
14/03/2012	11:30	Ravenhill 1st Presbyterian, Florida Street, Belfast
17/03/2012	10:00	Lá Fhéile Pádraig/Saint Patrick's Day, Irish Language Mass, Downpatrick
21/03/2012	11:00	Ballyhackamore Gospel Hall, Belfast
28/03/2012	10:30	Knockbreda Parish Church, Belfast
08/04/2012	11:00	Mary Mother of the Church, Saintfield and Carrickmannon
15/04/2012	10:00	Saint Peter's Cathedral (requiem for lost souls of *Titanic*)
17/04/2012	Unsure	Walking meditation with Thich Nhat Hanh, Stormont
22/04/2012	11:00	East End Baptist Church, Belfast
06/05/2012	11:00	Saint Louisa's, Chicago, USA
05/2012	Unsure	Baha'i House of Worship, Wilmette, Illinois, USA (visit not service)
05/2012	11:00	Old Saint Patrick's, Chicago, USA
03/06/2012	10:00	Ballyphilip and Ardquinn, Portaferry
10/06/2012	11:00	Glenburn Methodist Church, Belfast
17/06/2012	11:00	Whitewell Metropolitan Tabernacle, Belfast
06/07/2012	Noon	Saint Matthew's, Belfast
15/07/2012	11:30	Saint Canice's Cathedral, Kilkenny, Ireland
05/08/2012	11:30	Saint Joseph's, Clifden, Galway
12/08/2012	11:30	Mersey Street Presbyterian, Belfast
05/08/2012	09:00	Saint Ignatius Orthodox Church, Antrim Road (Grosvenor House)
09/08/2012	Unsure	Templemore Hall Assembly, Belfast
09/08/2012	1:00 PM	*Lament*, walking meditation with Suellen Semekoski
16/09/2012	11.30	Down Cathedral, Downpatrick
17/09/2012	10.30	Holy Cross Passionists, Belfast
20/09/2012	1:00 PM	Saint Anne's Cathedral (Divine Healing Service)
21/09/2012	Unsure	Stormont grounds (anniversary of the Ulster Covenant)
05/10/2012	1:00 PM.	Saint Anne's Cathedral (Divine Healing Service)
07/10/2012	11:00	Saint Jude's, Belfast
14/10/2012	11:00	Ballynafeigh Methodist Church, Belfast
16/10/2012	Unsure	Saint Matthew's, Belfast
23/10/2012	10:00	Holy Cross Passionists, Belfast
28/10/2012	10:45	Quaker Meeting House, south Belfast
04/11/2012	6:30 PM	Belfast Spiritualist Church, Lisburn Road, Belfast
21/11/2012	10:00	Knockbreda Methodist Church, Belfast
Unsure	2 days	Miranda Macpherson Retreat (Tobar Mhuire, Crossgar)
28/11/2012	10:00	Christian Fellowship Church (CFC), Belmont
01/12/2012	09:30	Clonard Monastery, Belfast
08/12/2012	Evening	Merci Marie, Lyon (festival of light)
11/12/2012	10:00	Cathédrale Notre-Dame de Paris, Paris, France
24/12/2012	9:00 PM	Saint Peter's Cathedral, Belfast (Midnight Mass)
06/01/2013	11:00	Fitzroy Presbyterian Church, Belfast
11/01/2013	1:00 PM	Saint Anne's Cathedral, Belfast (Divine Healing Service)
27/01/2013	11:00	Crescent Church, Belfast
Imbolc	7:00 PM	Women's meditation group, North Coast
02/02/2013	11:00	Crumlin Road Presbyterian, Belfast
09/02/2013	10:15	Kingdom Hall of Jehovah's Witnesses, Antrim Road, Belfast
03/03/2013	10:00	Saint Matthias' Parish of Saint Theresa, Belfast

10/03/2013	11:30	Knock Presbyterian, Belfast
17/03/2013	11:30	Saint Donard's Church of Ireland, Belfast (Saint Patrick's Day)
24/03/2013	10:30	Saint Brigid's, Belfast (Palm Sunday)
31/03/2013	11:30	Down Cathedral, Downpatrick (Easter service)
07/04/2013	11:30	Garnerville Presbyterian Church, Belfast
13/04/2013	All day	Potala Buddhist Centre, Belfast
14/04/2013	11:30	Knocknagoney Church of Ireland, Belfast
05/04/2013	1:00 PM	Saint Anne's Cathedral, Belfast (Divine Healing Service)
21/04/2013	11:30	Bloomfield Independent Methodist Church, Belfast
05/05/2013	11:00	Bloomfield Methodist Church, Belfast
10/05/2013	1:00 PM	Saint Anne's Cathedral, Belfast (Divine Healing Service)
12/05/2013	11:00	Dundonald Elim, Belfast
14/05/2013	3 days	Miranda Macpherson Retreat (Tobar Mhuire, Crossgar)
19/05/2013	11:00	Saint Joseph's, Sailortown, Belfast
09/06/2013	11:00	Belvoir Parish Church of Ireland, Belfast
23/06/2013	11:00	Fisherwick Presbyterian Church, Belfast
07/2013	11:00	Down Cathedral, Downpatrick
14/07/2013	10:00	Christ Church, Ballyculter
23/07/2013	10:00	Saint Patrick's, Donegall Street, Belfast
02/08/2013	1:00 PM	Saint Anne's Cathedral, Belfast (Divine Healing Service)
04/08/2013	11:00	Glencraig Church of Ireland, Holywood
16/08/2013	1:00 PM	Saint Anne's Cathedral, Belfast (Divine Healing Service)
23/08/2013	1:00 PM	Saint Anne's Cathedral, Belfast (Divine Healing Service)
25/08/2013	10:45	Strandtown Baptist, Belfast
06/09/2013	1:00 PM	Saint Anne's Cathedral, Belfast (Divine Healing Service)
15/09/2013	11:30	Stranmillis Evangelical Presbyterian, Belfast
28/09/2013	1 day	Sweat Lodge, Wicklow Mountains
11/09/2013	1:00 PM.	Saint Anne's Cathedral, Belfast (Divine Healing Service)
13/09/2013	7:30p.m	Saint Philip and Saint James, Holywood (harvest)
20/09/2013	11:30	Garnerville Presbyterian Church, Belfast
13/10/2013	11:00	Saint Philip and Saint James, Holywood
01/11/2013	11:00	Shankill Gospel Hall, Belfast
01/12/2013	11:00	Urban Village Church (Wicker Park), Chicago, USA
06/12/2013	6:00 PM	Taizé, Chicago, USA
07/12/2013	Unsure	Suellen's Sangha, Chicago, USA
24/12/2013	9:30 PM	Saint Peter's Cathedral, Belfast (Midnight Mass)
15/01/2014	Unsure	Wake Up to Love, Belfast City Hall walking meditation
16/01/2014	11:00	Rosemary Street Presbyterian, Belfast
02/02/2014	11:30	Crumlin Road Presbyterian, Belfast
09/02/2014	10:15	Kingdom Hall of Jehovah's Witnesses, Antrim Road, Belfast
06/02/2014	2:30 PM	Saint Dorothea's Church, Belfast (funeral)
09/03/2014	11:00	New Life City Church, Northumberland Street, Belfast
16/03/2014	Unsure	Saint Patrick's, Ballymacarret
30/03/2014	Noon	Saint Mary's, city centre, Belfast
19/04/2014	7:30 PM	Saint Mary Star of the Sea, Strangford
20/04/2014	10:00	Saint Patrick's, Saul (Easter service)
27/04/2014	8:30	Benburb Priory, Benburb
30/04/2014	1:00 PM	Saint Mary's, Belfast
04/05/2014	11:00	Sacred Heart Parish, Belfast
25/05/2014	09:00	Isaheen and Upper Moville, Donegal
08/06/2014	11:00	All Saints Church, Belfast

05/07/2014	11:00	Shankill Methodist Church, Belfast
12/07/2014	11:00	Woodvale Presbyterian Church, Belfast
31/09/2014	10:30	First Presbyterian Church, Rosemary Street, Belfast
04/10/2014	All day	Paul Burke Shaman, Donegal
05/10/2014	3:00 PM	Moneyreagh and Mountpottinger Non-Subscribing Presbyterian,
12/10/2014	11:30	Saint Mary Magdalene, Donegall Pass, Belfast
17/10/2014	1:00 PM	Saint Anne's Cathedral, Belfast (Divine Healing Service)
05/11/2014	4-day	Blue Cliff Monastery, New York, USA Veterans retreat
02/11/2014	1:00 PM	Saint Anne's Cathedral, Belfast (Divine Healing Service)
23/11/2014	10:30	Saint Bartholomew's, Stranmillis, Belfast
30/11/2014	11:00	Together in Spirit group
05/12/2014	1:00 PM	Saint Anne's Cathedral, Belfast (Divine Healing Service)
07/12/2014	10.30	Redeemer Central, Belfast
14/12/2014	11	Life Church, Belfast
21/12/2014	Noon	Saint Mathew's Church, Belfast
21/12/2014	6:00 PM	Knock Presbyterian Church, Belfast (Community Carol Service)
24/12/2014	8:00 PM	Saint Anne's Cathedral, Belfast (Lessons and Carols for Christmas)
04/01/2015	11	Jennymount Methodist, Belfast
09/01/2015	1:00 PM	Saint Anne's Cathedral, Belfast (Divine Healing Service)
10/01/2015	All day	Spiritual Psychology Course
11/01/2015	11:00	Together in Spirit group
17/01/2015	Unsure	*Corners of the Circle* art piece
18/01/2015	11:00	Saint Nicholas' Parish Church, Belfast
01/02/2015	11:00	Together in Spirit group
08/02/2015	11:00	Saint Nicholas' Parish Church, Belfast (baptism and confirmation)
09/02/2015	7:00 PM	Slighe na Beatha, Celtic Psalm singers at Skainos
11/02/2015	11:00	Church of the Nativity, Poleglass (confirmation)
13/02/2015	1:00 PM	Saint Anne's Cathedral, Belfast (Divine Healing Service)
15/02/1015	10:00	Christ Church, Ballyculter
22/02/2015	11:00	Jennymount Methodist, Belfast (christening)
16/03/2015	7:00 PM	Black Mountain Zen Centre, Belfast
17/03/2015	11:30	Down Cathedral, Downpatrick (Saint Patrick's Day with the Archbishop of Canterbury)
22/03/2015	08:30	Saint Agnes', Andersonstown Road, Belfast
28/03/2015	Unsure	*Corners of the Circle* performative bus trip
04/2015	2 days	Corrymeela Mindfulness retreat (sister Moon and sister Insight)
02/04/2015	6:30 PM	Saint Malachy's, Belfast (Holy Thursday)
03/04/2015	10:00	The Passion Walk, Belfast city centre (Good Friday)
05/04/2015	10:00	Saint Patrick's Memorial Church, Saul (Easter Sunday)
Unsure	7:00 PM	Black Mountain Zen Centre, Belfast (Paul Haller)
10/04/2015	11:00.	Saint Peter's Square, Rome, Italy
13/04/2015	6:00 PM	San Giuseppe alla Lungara, Rome, Italy
15/04/2015	11:00	Saint Peter's Square, Rome, Italy
17/04/2015	Evening	Saint Ignatio, Rome, Italy
26/04/2015	10:00	Malvern Assembly, Shankill Road, Belfast
10/05/2015	11:30	Saint Malachy's, Belfast
12/05/2015	2 days	Miranda Macpherson retreat (Tobar Mhuire, Crossgar)
17/05/2015	11:30	Saint Matthew's, Shankill, Belfast
22/05/2015	1:00 PM	Saint Anne's Cathedral, Belfast (Divine Healing Service)

24/05/2015	11:00	Christ Church Cathedral, Dublin
31/05/2015	11:30	Christ Church, Ballyculter
21/06/2015	11:00	Saint Patrick's Church of Ireland, Ballymacarrett
28/06/2015	11:00	Saint Patrick's Church of Ireland, Ballymacarrett
05/07/2015	11:00	Saint Patrick's, Portaferry
12/07/2015	11:30	Willowfield Parish Church, Belfast
30/08/2015	11:00	Saint Patrick's Church of Ireland, Ballymacarrett
06/09/2015	11:00	Malone Presbyterian, Belfast
18/10/2015	1:00 PM	Saint Anne's Cathedral, Belfast (Divine Healing Service)
18/10/2015	6:00 PM	Saint George's Parish Church, Belfast (sung service for Culture Night)
20/10/2015	11:00	Elim Pentecostal, Ravenhill Road, Belfast
27/10/2015	11:00	Saint Peter and Saint James, Belfast (harvest)
04/10/2015	10:30	Love International, Shaftsbury Square, Belfast
07/10/2015	10:25	Kirkwood Funeral Home, Belfast (funeral)
11/10/2015	11:00	Fortwilliam and Macrory Presbyterian, Belfast (harvest) (now closed)
18/10/2015	10:30	New Life City Church, Belfast
05/11/2015	11:30	Saint John's Parish, Falls Road, Belfast
22/11/2015	11:30	Braniel Methodist and Presbyterian Church, Belfast
29/11/2015	11:30	Holy Family, north Belfast
06/12/2015	09:30	Saint Gerard's, Antrim Road, Belfast
08/12/2015	6:30 PM	Saint Anne's Cathedral, Belfast (carols by candlelight service)
18/12/2015	1:00 PM	Saint Anne's Cathedral, Belfast (Divine Healing Service)
20/12/2015	11:30	Knock Evangelical Presbyterian, Belfast
01/01/2016	1:00 PM	Saint Mary's, Chapel Lane, Belfast
03/01/2016	11:00	Beersbridge Elim Church, Belfast
10/01/2016	11:30	Grove Baptist Church, Beersbridge Road, Belfast
17/01/2016	11:00	Saintfield Road Presbyterian, Belfast
21/01/2016	1:00 PM	Shaftsbury Square Reformed Presbyterian, Belfast
22/01/2016	1:00 PM	Saint Anne's Cathedral, Belfast (Divine Healing Service)
24/01/2016	11:00	Christ Church Presbyterian, Dundonald
30/01/2016	6.30p.m	Carryduff and Drumbo Parish Church, Belfast
07/02/2016	11:00	Dundonald Methodist, Belfast
14/02/2016	10:30	Vineyard at Fleming Fulton, Belfast
19/02/2016	1:00 PM	Saint Anne's Cathedral, Belfast (Divine Healing Service)
21/02/2016	10:00	Saint Anne's, Kilwee
28/02/2016	11:30	Hope Fellowship, Somerton Road, Belfast
06/03/2016	10:00	Belvoir Methodist Church, Belfast
16/03/2016	09:30	Saint Bernadette's, Belfast
17/03/2016	11:30	Down Cathedral, Downpatrick
20/03/2016	11:00	Eglinton Presbyterian, Ballysillan, Belfast
26/03/2016	10:00	Adoration Chapel, Falls Road, Belfast
27/03/2016	10:00	Holy Cross Church, Dunfanaghy, Donegal
11/04/2016	1:30 PM	Salvation Army Belfast Temple, Cregagh Road, Belfast
16/04/2016	1:00 PM	Saint Anne's Cathedral, Belfast (Divine Healing Service)
18/04/2016	10:00	Christ Church, Ballyculter
22/04/2016	1:00 PM	Saint Anne's Cathedral, Belfast (Divine Healing Service)
24/04/2016	11:00	Saint Stephen's, Millfield, Belfast
06/05/2016	1:00 PM	Saint Anne's Cathedral, Belfast (Divine Healing Service)
13/05/2016	1:00 PM	Saint Anne's Cathedral, Belfast (Divine Healing Service)
15/05/2016	11:00	Saint Patrick's Church of Ireland, Ballymacarret
05/06/2016	11:00	Saint Patrick's, Ballyphilip, Portaferry

12/06/2016	09:30	Christian Fellowship Church (CFC), Belmont
16/06/2016	11:00	Soka Gakkai, Greyabbey Sanga
22/06/2016	09:15	Saint Mark's, Ballysillan, Belfast
03/07/2016	11:00	Saint Patrick's Church of Ireland, Ballymacarret (flower festival)
05/07/2016	11:00	Portaferry Presbyterian, Portaferry
11/07/2016	10:00	Saint Cooey's Wells, Portaferry (confirmation)
11/07/2016	3:00 PM	Roselawn, Belfast (humanist funeral)
12/07/2016	10:00	Soka Gakkai International Buddhists Regional Meeting, Farset
19/07/2016	10:00	The Village, Newtownards Road (formally Bloomfield Baptist)
24/07/2016	1:00 PM	Saint Anne's Cathedral, Belfast (Divine Healing Service)
26/07/2016	11:00	Castlereagh Gospel Hall, Belfast
01/08/2016	11:00	Saint Patrick's, Ballymacarret, hundred-year Somme commemoration service
29/09/2016	11:00	Joanmount Methodist, Belfast
04/10/2016	11:00	Saint Michael the Archangel, Andersonstown, Belfast
11/10/2016	11:30	Great Victoria Street Baptist Church, Belfast
18/10/2016	11:30	Sinclair Seaman's Presbyterian Church, Belfast
14/11/2016	11:00	Portico, Portaferry (humanist funeral)
16/11/2016	7:00 PM	Ballybeen Gospel Hall, Belfast
23/11/2016	11:00	Agāpé Centre, Lisburn Road, Belfast
04/12/2016	11:00	Gospel Hall, Limestone Road, Belfast
09/12/2016	7:30 PM	Saint Anne's Cathedral, Belfast (carols by candlelight)
11/12/2016	11:30	Westbourne Presbyterian, Belfast
18/12/2016	6:30 PM	Knock Presbyterian Church (community carol service)
25/12/2016	10:30	Temple Réformé à Nyons, France
01/01/2017	11:30	Saint Philip and Saint James, Holywood
15/01/2017	11:30	Saint Michael's, Shankill Road, Belfast
30/01/2017	11:00	Ballysillan Elim Church, Belfast
05/02/2017	09:55	Saint Vincent de Paul, Ligoniel (confirmation)
07/02/2017	7:30 PM	Harmony and healing, interfaith encounter and celebration, Grosvenor Hall, Belfast
12/02/2017	11:00	McCracken Memorial Presbyterian, Belfast
27/02/2017	11:00	Saint Katherine's, Dunlambert Park, Belfast
17/03/2017	09:30	Saint Patrick's Memorial Church, Saul
17/03/2017	11:45	Down Cathedral, Downpatrick (Saint Patrick's Day)
19/03/2017	11:00	Belvoir Presbyterian, Belfast
26/03/2017	11:30	Gilnahirk Presbyterian, Belfast
02/04/2017	11:00	Crosspoint church, Dundonald
12/04/2017	1:00 PM	Saint Anne's Cathedral, Belfast (Divine Healing Service)
14/04/2017	7:30 PM	Portaferry Presbyterian (Tenenbrae service, NewQuay Singers)
16/04/2017	10:00	Saint Patrick's Memorial Church, Saul
23/04/2017	11:00	Forestside Christian Centre, Belvoir
04/05/2017	1:00 PM	Saint Anne's Cathedral, Belfast (Divine Healing Service)
14/05/2017	11:00	Saint Mary's, Chapel Lane, Belfast (Irish Language service)
18/05/2017	Noon	John Smyth Funeral Home (humanist funeral)
21/05/2017	7:00 PM	Abundant Grace Christian Assembly, Duncairn Gardens, Belfast
29/05/2017	10:00	Portaferry Presbyterian, Portaferry
22/06/2017	1:00 PM	Saint Anne's Cathedral, Belfast (Divine Healing Service)
17/06/2017	11:00	Redeemer Central, Belfast

Date	Time	Venue
01/07/2017	11:00	Ava Street Pentecostal Church, Belfast
07/08/2017	1:00 PM	Saint Anne's Cathedral, Belfast (Divine Healing Service)
13/08/2017	Noon	Church of Perpetual Adoration, Falls Road, Belfast
16/08/2017	11:00	Shankill Baptist, Belfast
30/08/2017	11:30	West Kirk Presbyterian, Shankill Road, Belfast
06/08/2017	Noon	Saint Oliver Plunkett, Paróiste Naomh Oilibhéar Pluincéid
20/08/2017	10:00	Saint Patrick's Memorial Church, Saul
28/08/2017	Noon	Church of Perpetual Adoration, Falls Road, Belfast
01/09/2017	1:00 PM	Saint Anne's Cathedral, Belfast (Divine Healing Service)
03/09/2017	11:30	Cairnshill Methodist, Saintfield Road, Belfast
08/09/2017	1:00 PM	Saint Anne's Cathedral, Belfast (Divine Healing Service)
10/09/2017	11:30	John White Memorial, Tennent Street, Belfast
17/09/2017	11:00	Living Room Church, Carlisle Circus, Belfast
01/10/2017	10:00	Saint Patrick's Memorial Church, Saul
08/10/2017	10:30	Church on the Green, Dundonald Presbyterian, Belfast
15/10/2017	11:30	Dundonald Baptist, Belfast
29/10/2017	11:30	Coastlands Elim, Holywood
18/11/2017	1:00 PM	Saint Anne's Cathedral, Belfast (Divine Healing Service)
19/11/2017	11:00	Saint Mary's, Ballybeen, Belfast
03/12/2017	11:30	Townsend Street Presbyterian, Belfast
09/12/2017	1:00 PM	Saint Anne's Cathedral, Belfast (Divine Healing Service)
10/12/2017	9:00 PM	Queen's University carol service (Great Hall)
17/12/2017	08:30	Saint George's Eucharist, Belfast
23/12/2017	7:30 PM	Portaferry Presbyterian, Portaferry (carol service, NewQuay singers)
01/01/2018	Noon	Adoration Chapel, Falls Road, Belfast
05/01/2018	1:00 PM	Saint Anne's Cathedral, Belfast (Divine Healing Service)
07/01/2018	11:00	Eastpoint Church, Tullycarnet, Belfast
12/01/2018	09:30	Clonard Monastery, Belfast
19/01/2018	1:00 PM	Saint Anne's Cathedral, Belfast (Divine Healing Service)
21/01/2018	11:30	Donegall Road Methodist Church, Belfast
28/01/2018	6:30 PM	Centre Church, Berry Street, Belfast
04/02/2018	11:30	Great Victoria Street Presbyterian Church, Belfast
11/02/2018	11:00	Saint Simon's, Donegall Road, Belfast
14/02/2018	1:00 PM	Saint George's Church, Belfast (Ash Wednesday)
16/2/2018	1:00 PM	Saint Anne's Cathedral, Belfast (Divine Healing Service)
18/2/2018	10:00	Moravian Church, University Road, Belfast
Unsure	All day	Spirit of Macha, Navan Fort
24/02/2018	10:00	Christ Church, Ballyculter
04/03/2018	7:30 PM	Glenmachan Church of God, Belfast
11/03/2018	11:30	Seymour Hill Methodist Church, Belfast
14/03/2018	09:30	Clonard Monastery, Belfast (Saint Patrick's Day service)
16/03/2018	1:00 PM	Saint Anne's Cathedral, Belfast (Divine Healing Service)
18/03/2018	10:00	Ballyphilip and Ardquinn, Portaferry
25/03/2018	11:00	Church of the Nazarene, Donegall Road, Belfast (Palm Sunday)
29/03/2018	7:00 PM	Portaferry Presbyterian, (Tenenbrae service, NewQuay Singers)
01/04/2018	06:45	Inch Abbey, Downpatrick (dawn service)
01/04/2018	09:30	Saint Patrick's, Saul
unsure	10:30	Pilates Maitri Studios, Belfast
08/05/2018	9:00 PM	Iona Abbey, Isle of Iona
09/05/2018	5:00 PM	Bishop's House, Isle of Iona
10/05/2018	9:00 PM	Iona Abbey, Isle of Iona

20/05/2018	10:00	Ballyphilip and Ardquinn, Portaferry (Pentecost)
20/05/2018	5:00 PM	Saint George's, Belfast, International Day Against Homophobia and Transphobia
10/06/2018	10:30	Mindfulness with Veronica Ellis, Maitri Studios
24/06/2018	10:00	Donegall Road Gospel Hall, Belfast
01/07/2018	10:00	Ballyphilip and Ardquinn, Portaferry
15/07/2018	11:00	Central (offshoot of Carnmoney Presbyterian), Assembly Buildings
22/07/2018	10:00	Ballyphilip and Ardquinn, Portaferry
05/08/2018	10:45	Methodist church, Fivemiletown
13/08/2018	7:00 PM	Leaves of the Tree Sangha, Ulster Hospital Chaplaincy
19/08/2018	11:00	Sandy Row Methodist, Belfast
26/08/2018	11:15	Ebenezer Gospel Hall, Belfast
31/08/2018	1:00 PM	Saint Anne's Cathedral, Belfast (Divine Healing Service)
02/09/2018	10:00	Cregagh Street Gospel Hall, Belfast
09/09/2018	All day	Veronica Ellis Mindfulness Retreat, Spa
16/09/2018	11:00	Dundonald Elim Pentecostal, Belfast
19/09/2018	Noon	Church of good Shepherd, Whiteabbey (funeral)
23/09/2018	7:00 PM	Laganvale Gospel Hall, Belfast
07/10/2018	11:30	All Souls Non-Subscribing Presbyterian, Belfast
14/10/2018	7:30 PM	Portaferry Presbyterian (Harvest Thanksgiving, NewQuay Singers)
26/10/2018	1:00 PM	Saint Anne's Cathedral, Belfast (Divine Healing Service)
28/10/2018	7:30 PM	The Ark Church, north Belfast
03/11/2018	5:30 PM	Winchester Cathedral, England (Choral Evening Song)
06/11/2018	10:00	Chalfont Saint Giles Parish Church, England
11/11/2018	11:30	John Knox Free Presbyterian, Belfast (Remembrance Sunday)
15/11/2018	7:30 PM	Soul Space, Duncairn Arts Centre, Belfast
18/11/2018	10:00	Saint Caelan's, Kilief
14/12/2018	1:00 PM	Saint Anne's Cathedral, Belfast (Divine Healing Service)
16/12/2018	11:00	Universal Church of the Kingdom of God, Belfast
16/12/2018	7:00 PM	Down Cathedral, Downpatrick (Carols by Candlelight)
22/12/2018	7:30 PM	Portaferry Presbyterian (Carols by Candlelight, NewQuay Singers)
25/12/2018	08:30	Old Court, Strangford
02/01/2019	1:00 PM	Saint Mary's, Belfast
06/01/2019	Noon	Saint Mary's, Greencastle
13/01/2019	11:00	Alexandra Presbyterian, Belfast
25/01/2019	1:00 PM	Saint Patrick's, Donegall Street, Belfast
27/01/2019	11:00	Alexandra Presbyterian, Belfast
01/02/2019	1:00 PM	Saint Anne's Cathedral, Belfast (Divine Healing Service)
03/02/2019	10:15	Saint Mary's University Chapel, Falls Road, Belfast
10/02/2019	08:30	Saint Thomas' Parish Church, Belfast
15/02/2019	1:00 PM	Saint Anne's Cathedral, Belfast (Divine Healing Service)
17/02/2019	1:45 PM	Saint John the Evangelist, Malone, Belfast
23/02/2019	2 days	Celtic Mindfulness, Navan Fort
03/03/2019	7:00 PM	The Dock Cafe, Titanic Quarter
06/03/2019	10:00	Saint Patrick's, Donegall Road, Belfast (Ash Wednesday service)
08/03/2019	1:00 PM	Saint Anne's Cathedral, Belfast (Divine Healing Service)
10/03/2019	11:00	Baptist Assembly, Albertbridge Road (now Kingdom Harvest Church)
14/03/2019	12:30	Saint Paul's Cathedral, London
17/03/2019	09:30	Clonard Monastery (Saint Patrick's Day)

18/03/2019	1:00 PM	Ballyphilip and Ardquinn, Portaferry (funeral service)
24/03/2019	10:00	Cliftonville Moravian Church, Belfast
07/04/2019	11:15	Gilnahirk Baptist Church, Belfast
14/04/2019	Noon	Saint John the Evangelist, Falls Road, Belfast (Palm Sunday)
18/04/2019	7:00 PM	Saint John the Evangelist, Falls Road, Belfast (Holy Thursday)
19/04/2019	7:30 PM	Portico, Portaferry (Tenenbrae Service Requiem, NewQuay Choir)
21/04/2019	06:15	Dawn service at Inch Abbey, Downpatrick
24/04/2019	1:00 PM	Saint Anne's Cathedral, Belfast (funeral)
28/04/2019	11:00	Foundation Church, Ashfield Girls' School, Belfast
30/04/2019	Noon	Saint Brigid's, Belfast (funeral)
19/05/2019	11:00	Castlereagh Baptist Church, Belfast
26/05/2019	10:00	Saint Caelan's, Kilclief
02/06/2019	11:30.	Saint Brendan's, Sydenham, Belfast
09/06/2019	10:30	Strand Church, Sydenham, Belfast
16/06/2019	10:30	Salvation Army, north Belfast, York Road
23/06/2019	11:00	Salvation Army, Ballybeen, Belfast
29/06/2019	All day	Healing workshop, Carlingford Heritage Museum (converted church)
07/07/2019	11:30	Knockbracken Congregational, Belfast
14/07/2019	1:00 PM	L'église Saint Timothée de Veauche Bourg, France (wedding)
11/08/2019	11:00	Salvation Army, Dublin Road, Belfast
01/09/2019	10:30	Belfast Church of Christ, Crescent Arts Centre, Belfast
08/09/2019	11:30	Calvary Baptist Church, Belfast
15/09/2019	11:00	The Church of God, Shankill Road, Belfast
22/09/2019	11:00	Shankill Community Fellowship, Belfast
28/09/2019	6:00 PM	Corpus Christi, Ballymurphy, Belfast
06/10/2019	11:00	Christian Fellowship Church (CFC) Inner East, Belfast
07/10/2019	Noon	Church of Adoration, Falls Road, Belfast
13/10/2019	11:30	Park Avenue Free Methodist Church, Belfast
16/10/2019	3:00 PM	Knock Presbyterian Church, Belfast (funeral)
20/10/2019	3:00 PM	Killyleagh Parish Church, Killyleagh (funeral)
20/10/2019	7:30 PM	Portaferry Presbyterian (NewQuay Singers, Harvest Thanksgiving)
27/10/2019	11:30	Re: Hope church, Malone Lodge Hotel
27/10/2019	6:30 PM	NewQuay Choir, 150-year celebration of Saint Saviour's Greyabbey Parish Church

Please note if you intend to visit any of the churches for a service please check times before hand.